D0777008

MISSING!

MYSTERIOUS CASES OF PEOPLE GONE MISSING THROUGH THE CENTURIES

MISSING!

MYSTERIOUS CASES

OF PEOPLE GONE MISSING THROUGH THE CENTURIES

WRITTEN AND ILLUSTRATED BY

Brenda Z. Guiberson

HENRY HOLT AND COMPANY
NEW YORK

Thanks to Laura Godwin, Julia Sooy, Christine Kettner, Patrick Collins, Tom Nau, Jennifer Healey, Sherri Schmidt, Barbara Bakowski, Valerie Shea, and all those who brought expertise to the many layers of this book.

Henry Holt and Company, *Publishers since 1866*
Henry Holt® is a registered trademark of Macmillan Publishing Group, LLC
175 Fifth Avenue, New York, New York 10010 • mackids.com

ISBN 978-1-250-13340-3
Library of Congress Control Number 2018936454

Our books may be purchased in bulk for promotional, educational, or business use. Please contact your local bookseller or the Macmillan Corporate and Premium Sales Department at (800) 221-7945 ext. 5442 or by e-mail at MacmillanSpecialMarkets@macmillan.com.

First edition, 2019 / Designed by Christine Kettner
Printed in the United States of America
by LSC Communications, Harrison, Virginia

10 9 8 7 6 5 4 3 2 1

*For a hopeful spirit and courage
to those waiting to hear*

CONTENTS

MISSING!

At any one moment, thousands of people might be missing. Some pop up after a period of time, and others are eventually found under tragic circumstances.

This book is not about those people. Instead it takes a look at an intriguing few who, after years, decades, and sometimes centuries of investigation, still leave unanswered questions. Family, friends, law enforcement, historians, and all who are curious want to know what happened. Books have been written, theories explored, and adventurous searches undertaken, but final proof about their fate remains just out of reach. In a fuzzy area of no conclusive facts, these missing can creep into the realm of mysterious legend, tantalizing myth, or wispy ghost stories.

Some of these people were already famous and had a huge effect on the lives and times around them. Others became famous only after they disappeared, and their missing status led to changes in such areas as politics and airplane construction.

Did you know that a man who tried to help truck drivers during the Great Depression found himself in deep trouble with dangerous mobsters? For decades, many investigators have followed clues to a possible burial site in such places as New Jersey's Giants Stadium and a Florida swamp.

Did you know that a hijacker who disappeared after parachuting from a plane left behind a clip-on tie that was recently discovered to contain new clues?

Did you know that a girl who knew all about commas and the alphabet at age two, and was typing at age three, soon became widely admired as a child novelist?

Did you know that President Franklin Roosevelt had a runway built on a tiny Pacific island for a famous aviator before she began a long flight around the world?

Did you know that a man was kidnapped after he announced a decision to publish secrets about an organization that turned out to be not so secret after all?

And did you know that two young princes went missing five hundred years ago during a long civil war in England? Someone in the royal family was responsible for their disappearance, but who? Were they murdered? Did either survive?

These stories begin with intrigue but are not quite finished. Acceptable proof to end them would be DNA evidence, fingerprints, a photo, a body, something very solid and not in dispute.

Meanwhile, the stories continue to swirl with new theories, adventurous searches, and reevaluations of old clues with new methods.

Every curious and determined investigator hopes to discover the final answer and be the person to end the mystery.

MISSING!

MYSTERIOUS CASES OF PEOPLE GONE MISSING THROUGH THE CENTURIES

CHAPTER 1

Jimmy Hoffa and the Truckers

*You almost had to live through it to really know the gut ripping
misery of the depression during the early thirties which led to
labor's bloodiest and most violent days.*
—*Jimmy Hoffa*

A BUSY CHILDHOOD

JIMMY WAS BORN on Valentine's Day 1913 in Brazil, Indiana—the third of four children. The father, John, was descended from German immigrants. In this coal country he operated a rig that drilled for coal samples deep in the earth. He was often traveling, and the children looked forward to his return. Jimmy recalled that "he played our games: hide 'n' seek, and tag, and marbles" and took them to "the drugstore for a phosphate drink." When the circus was in town, they went to see the clowns and animals, too.

Their mother, Viola Riddle Hoffa, stayed home, where she operated a laundry business. Jennetta helped with the washing and ironing. Jimmy and Billy picked up and returned bundles of clothing. Jimmy also split kindling for the kitchen stove and lugged water to keep the washing boiler full. Billy spent more time with the kitchen garden. Nancy, the youngest, dusted and cleaned. All had a standing order that "at the first sign of rain, no matter where we were, we had to make a beeline for the back yard and snatch clothing from the lines and get it inside."

In 1920, Jimmy's father returned home from his work one day very confused and unable to keep his balance. After several weeks in the hospital and no definite diagnosis, John died. Jimmy was seven.

Viola had enormous medical bills, and the rent was overdue. In

Jimmy Hoffa making a phone call to settle a strike.

a time of no welfare or aid to dependent children, the family moved in with their grandfather. Unfortunately, he also died within the year.

The children were expected to keep up with schoolwork along with the chores. The big event of the week was Sunday dinner. Billy and Jimmy sometimes helped to provide food. One Sunday, Billy and Jimmy were told to kill a fat chicken for dinner. Jimmy held the bird while Billy swung the ax. The ax hit Jimmy's hand and cut some tendons. Jimmy was rushed off to the doctor in a Model T Ford. The doctor said Jimmy might never be able to grasp with the hand, but he was determined. With a lot of pain and exercising, he regained full use of his hand after several months.

Looking for better opportunities, the family soon moved to nearby Clinton—a booming coal mining town that was becoming a center for bootlegging (making illegal alcohol). The Hoffas lived in a two-room house in the town's Little Italy neighborhood, where the Ku Klux Klan marched down the street to intimidate the Catholic immigrants, who were seen as un-American. Then there were the United Mine Workers strikes, shootouts with bootleggers, police raids, and other street skirmishes. In a time of lawlessness, Clinton was one of the roughest towns in the Midwest. Jimmy often witnessed violent clashes among these groups.

Meanwhile, the Hoffas had to pay the rent, which was six dollars a month. The laundry business did not provide enough money, especially when it rained. Viola was resourceful and found work as a

Jimmy (left) with his brother, Billy, in the 1920s.

waitress, a cook, and an ironer of sheets at the local hospital. But with a hungry family, she was always looking for better opportunities.

After about three years in this turbulent neighborhood, coal mines began to close and the laundry business slumped. The family moved to Detroit, where the automotive business was beginning to boom. Viola's first job was pressing clothes in a laundry. Then she got hired by Ternstedt, an automotive parts factory, to work on an assembly line with mostly Polish and Hungarian immigrants. She spent her time screwing a tap onto a threaded piece of metal that passed by on a conveyor belt.

In the 1920s, car and truck production was a booming industry. Here, final assembled models and one body frame are displayed in a Ford showroom.
[Library of Congress]

BOOM TIMES AND BUST

After four years, Viola moved on to polishing radiator caps. Sometimes she was laid off. "She never whimpered, never cried and never let anyone cry in front of her," Jimmy recalled. "She'd give 'em a whack."

To help out, Jimmy worked at a grocery unloading trucks and doing other odd jobs. The money went to his mother. He kept up with his schoolwork with B grades, but his best class was gym. He won medals in the decathlon and said his muscles gave "a sort of itching or pressuring telling me they have to be exercised." Unlike his six-foot father, Jimmy was short, five feet five, but he was very strong. All through his life he did seventy-five push-ups a day and lifted weights.

When Jimmy graduated from the ninth grade, he decided to work full-time and not return to school. He was fourteen. He got a job at Frank & Cedar's Dry Goods and General Merchandise and was paid two dollars a day. He also got an employee discount. On advice from his mother, he bought a few clothes.

For the first time since early childhood, Jimmy had extra hours for leisure. He played sandlot baseball and went fishing. When the fish weren't biting, he walked for miles along the lakeshore and got to know the birds and where they nested. He identified edible plants like black birch, sassafras root, and wintergreen. Looking back years later, he remarked that he was glad that despite rapid industrialization, with so many factories, trucks, and trains, there were still places set aside for nature lovers.

Jimmy and his family were like many others in the 1920s who moved from the country to the city looking for a steady job. If they found it, they used new kinds of credit to buy cars and appliances. Some even bought stocks. A very tiny wealthy group was making a huge fortune in the stock market.

Jimmy had a fairly good job at the department store. Then the stock market crashed in 1929. As things got worse and the Great Depression set in, people quit buying clothes and other niceties. Many employees were getting laid off. By the end of 1930, Detroit had an unemployment rate of nearly 33 percent, the highest of any major city. One social worker wrote that many "automobile workers were to be found among the men and women shuffling dejectedly at the public and private employment offices . . . and in those lines which run into the thousands before the gate [of] any of the large plants which are hiring help."

At age sixteen, Jimmy began to look for more stable work.

JIMMY AND THE STRAWBERRY BOYS

A friend of Jimmy's advised him to get into the food business. "People have to eat no matter what," he said. Because Jimmy looked strong and said he was eighteen, he managed to land a job with the Kroger Grocery and Baking Company, loading and unloading fresh fruits and vegetables from railcars onto trucks.

Jimmy showed up with other workers at 5:00 p.m. for the twelve-hour night shift. As in other places across the country, hundreds of desperate people waited in line outside the Kroger gate. All were hoping someone would get fired or sick so they could have that job.

Kroger wages were thirty-two cents per hour. However, employees were paid only if they were actually unloading a boxcar or loading an order onto trucks. If there was no cargo at the platform, the men were still required to stick around, sometimes for hours, with no pay. When a shipment did arrive, Jimmy was in awe of it all. Watermelons came in from Florida, eggs from Delaware, cherries from Michigan, lettuce and asparagus from California, apples from Oregon, and cantaloupes from Arizona.

All of this colorful beauty was ruined by a platform boss resented for his "outrageous meanness." Since there were no regular work rules, the foreman could make them up as he pleased. He abused and threatened people and always had a triumphant smile when he managed to get rid of workers, usually without cause. He fired people to make room for a friend, or the son of a friend, or just because he felt like it.

Jimmy wrote that this man was "the kind of guy who causes unions."

Trucks from all over the country loaded up at small farms to bring produce
to the markets. [Library of Congress]

The workers wanted the boss to treat them fairly, and they also
wanted a better pay guarantee. What if Kroger would guarantee at
least four hours' pay for a twelve-hour shift?

One man, Sam Calhoun, urged the workers to unionize, to all
come together to work for a common cause. "If we didn't organize, we
knew, our lives would be miserable," Jimmy wrote. "One by one we
would be fired for no reason."

Most workers were wary of taking action. Would they have to go on strike to get any recognition? Would the company bring in strike-breakers to work in their place? Would their employer hire thugs, or goon squads, to rough them up with nightsticks? And what if they lost their jobs?

To deal with these concerns, Jimmy used the idle periods when they were not being paid to talk quietly with others and develop a plan. Most workers didn't want to ask for too much. They just wanted someone to listen to them.

Then an event occurred that brought all the workers together. In the spring of 1931, two men left the warehouse to get a meal from a dinner cart. This was the usual custom. However, the foreman went outside and hired two from the unemployed line. When the two mid-night snackers returned, they found the gate locked and learned that they no longer worked for Kroger. This incident was witnessed by all 175 employees on the night shift. Now they were really mad and 100 percent in favor of a strike. But how? And when?

Jimmy suggested they wait for some expensive perishables to come in. This would hit the company in the pocketbook. Four days later some boxcars arrived dripping melted ice. Inside were luscious red strawberries. Jimmy gave a signal, and the workers stopped loading the strawberries into the trucks. The foreman was furious, but the crew chanted for the night manager, who came out of his office.

Jimmy said they had a list of grievances to talk about and would like a meeting. Rather than let the expensive produce go to waste, the manager agreed to meet with Jimmy and representatives of the

Strawberry Boys. They successfully gained better wages and some working rules for the foreman. But there was a limit. The company only gave them a one-year contract.

This was good enough for Jimmy. He had just taken his first step to becoming a powerful union leader.

> ## "HI, I'M JIMMYHOFFAORGANIZERFORTHE TEAMSTERS, ANDIWONDERIFICOULD TALKTOYOU."

Beginning in 1933, Congress passed laws guaranteeing employees the right to organize and bargain collectively, protecting them from interference or being fired if they wanted to unionize. Jimmy, however, continued to be hassled at Kroger because of union activities. He finally quit, about the same time that he was fired.

Almost immediately he was invited by officials in the International Brotherhood of Teamsters to become an organizer with Local 299 in Detroit. The Detroit Teamsters union had just 250 members and was running out of money. It was known for using threats and bombings and had been placed in a trusteeship, which meant it had an overseer and no elections. The union had managed to get a 10 percent raise for its members, but the truckers were still making poverty-level wages.

Jimmy's job was to improve the finances and sign up new

members. The Teamsters at that time represented mostly short-haul drivers making local deliveries. Jimmy worked with these current members in the city, but he also wanted to sign up long-haul drivers who spent overlong hours on the new highways being built across the country. One driver said he had worked "5 days, from 2 p.m. Sunday to 5 a.m. Saturday. In that time I got not over 14 hours' sleep."

Jimmy started out by approaching truck drivers at their work. But the employers drove him off, or the truckers wouldn't talk to him because they were afraid of losing their jobs.

Jimmy looked for a better way to make contact. He knew the long-haul drivers needed breaks and sometimes parked on the edges of the highways for a quick snooze. So Jimmy set out to find them.

He drove around looking for parked trucks on Ontario's Highway 2 between Detroit and Buffalo, on old U.S. Highway 6 on the way to Cleveland, or on U.S. 112 to and from Chicago. He knocked on windows, hoping to get a moment to connect with exhausted drivers. It was dangerous work. The drivers often woke up with a tire iron or wrench in their hands, ready to hit first and ask questions later. Jimmy learned to talk fast and then back up quickly.

"Hi,I'mJimmyHoffaOrganizerfortheTeamsters,andIwonderifI couldtalktoyou."

Once awake, the drivers revealed many reservations about a union. Some were very independent and wanted to be in charge themselves. What if they joined up and then got fired? And wasn't a union

Jimmy had to talk fast when he approached truck drivers snoozing
on the side of highways.

unpatriotic? Or a secret lodge? And union dues? Who had money for
that?

Jimmy learned to come up with quick answers. He would tell
them that many were joining. Soon they could look forward to pay
raises and better working conditions. And there would be meetings
where they could vote on decisions. The union bosses would be working for them.

He talked about lack of adequate overtime, no minimum safety
standards, no recognition of highway fatigue. These conversations on
the highways led to many sign-ups.

Then Jimmy met a goon squad. One night he rapped on a truck door, but it wasn't a driver who came out. It was two "burly thugs" carrying "snappers," flexible billy clubs with lead weights in the ends. Hired by an employer, they bashed Jimmy around. Then they snarled out a message: "Stay away from our trucks! This is just a warning. Next time it'll be first class."

For safety, Jimmy and other union organizers started to go out in pairs. The police began to stop them for motor-vehicle violations and searched their vehicles. They took away tire irons and anything that could be used as a weapon or protection. Union workers spent hours in court, using up union money, for going too fast past a school, failing to slow down, driving to the left of a white line. More than one hundred organizers ended up in the hospital, where they were sometimes required to pay cash in advance for emergency treatment.

Jimmy said that his "scalp was laid open sufficiently wide to require stitches no less than six times during the first year I was Business Agent of Local 299. I was beaten up by cops or strikebreakers at least two dozen times that year."

STITCHES, STRIKES, AND HEADING OUT OF POVERTY

Jimmy used picket lines, strikes, and threats to stop deliveries in order to get employers to recognize the union. Sometimes he and others were arrested. In one twenty-four-hour period on a picket line he was taken to jail eighteen times but never charged with anything. The sergeant who arrested Jimmy said he brought him in before he could make trouble. The police captain had to release Jimmy each time because he had not caused any problems. Jimmy eventually ran out of money to take the bus back to the picket line and borrowed a dime from the sergeant. All the people on the picket line were impressed that Jimmy kept returning.

As the country went into a deep depression and lost its economic balance, union organizers were considered troublemakers or communists. At one point, the son of an employer showed up looking for Hoffa and shot his brother, Billy, in error. Billy survived.

But gradually more and more employees and owners of small businesses began to support union activities. According to Jimmy, "If a worker is to be totally responsible to his employer, then the employer must be totally responsible to his worker." Workers in the garment, laundry, steel, railroad, bakery, and other industries were all using strikes and picket lines to improve their working conditions.

Jimmy focused on getting better wages and working conditions for the truck drivers. By 1936, the carhaul members (including the truck drivers) in Local 299 had entered the middle class with wages raised by 30 percent. He also supported picket lines and work stoppages for other workers such as the United Auto Workers and the Polish women who shut down twelve laundries to demand union recognition.

Teamsters holding picket signs to support better working conditions for other workers in 1954. [Library of Congress]

He met his wife, Josephine Poszywak, on that picket line. They eventually had two children—James and Barbara. Jimmy was devoted to his family and never smoked or drank. He was a voracious reader, mostly of economics and politics.

But most of the time Jimmy was at work, where he had so many types of truck drivers to reach. There were short-haul, long-haul, and drive-away drivers who took the new cars out of Detroit to places in the country. There were milk drivers, van drivers, cab drivers, and general drivers, too. Jimmy reached out to all of them. In 1937, Local 299 and other locals helped trucking companies get reduced license-plate and mileage fees with hopes that the drivers would benefit with higher wages. This did not happen, which led to more strikes. Eventually, most truckers gained higher wages.

Over the decades, as Jimmy worked his way up to president of the International Brotherhood of Teamsters, he built the organization from seventy-five thousand members across the country to over 1.8 million. He became the leader of the most powerful union in the nation. What if Jimmy called a general strike to stop all trucks? Such an action could shut down deliveries across the country.

Jimmy liked publicity, was well known, and was often on television. Many feared his power. As Jimmy said, "If you got it, . . . a truck driver brought it to you. . . . That's the whole secret to what we do." Deliveries included food, clothing, medicine, building materials, and fuel.

CRIME AND TROUBLE

In building up the Teamsters' membership, Jimmy sometimes used strong-arm tactics to fight off bids from other unions competing for territory and power. At one point he may have sought an alliance with a Detroit crime family headed by Santo "the Shark" Perrone. His organization helped out with "car chases, shoot-outs, and sprawling

MILK TRUCKERS DO NOT !

PICK UP MILK AT FARMS WHERE THERE ARE CASES OF DIPHTHERIA

SCARLET FEVER
INFANTILE PARALYSIS
SPINAL MENINGITIS
SMALLPOX TYPHOID

Report all cases on your route to . . . .

FOOD and DRUG ADMINSTRATION
ROOM 11 · · CITY HALL
CLEVELAND, O., MA 4600

fistfights," sometimes as "hired muscle for Detroit's management," according to Charles Brandt, a former prosecutor turned author.

Jimmy's goal was always to get better wages and working conditions for the Teamsters. In 1955, he created the Central States Pension Fund. With this system, Teamsters could build up a nest egg with contributions from their employer that would guarantee them an income when they retired. Unions all over the country followed this model, and Jimmy became a hero to working people.

This pension fund put millions of dollars under Jimmy's control. He made loans from it and charged interest, and the money was paid back. This might have been a good business decision except . . .

Jimmy made some of these loans to a criminal group of people called La Cosa Nostra, who had dangerous, treacherous, and murderous methods for conducting business.

THE CRIMINAL BUSINESS OF LA COSA NOSTRA

La Cosa Nostra means "this thing of ours." It had other names, too, like the mob, the Mafia, and organized crime. With few exceptions, members of the Mafia were Italians who had been born into this life. It was a group that valued secrecy. No one really knew for sure how big it was until November 14, 1957, one month after Jimmy was elected national president of the Teamsters union.

"Sure you got everything under control, Jimmy?"
[A 1957 Herblock Cartoon. © The Herb Block Foundation]

On October 25, 1957, Albert Anastasia, "the Lord High Exe-cutioner," was shot in Manhattan while sitting in a barber's chair with a hot towel over his face. Other members of the Mafia had also been killed while Vito Genovese took control of one of the New York mob families. These were rogue killings, as it had been a mob rule that no one could be eliminated unless everyone agreed to it. From all over the country mob bosses drove their luxurious cars to the home of Joseph "Joe the Barber" Barbara in Apalachin, New York, to discuss the situation.

Two New York state troopers happened to see Barbara's son requesting a block of rooms at a motel and discovered the meeting. The officers showed up at the mansion the next day and started to take down the license plate numbers of all the expensive out-of-state cars. Barbara's wife spotted them, and more than a hundred mob bosses panicked. They quickly ran into the woods or ducked into the basement, but fifty-eight mobsters were caught and arrested.

Across the country people were shocked. For the first time the FBI could see that there was a vast network of gangsters. They had carved America into twenty-four territories and worked together to use brutal and violent means to conduct business. These methods included arson, bombings, beatings, acid attacks, and murder.

Santo "the Shark" Perrone was part of this violent gangland network, many of whose members would end up murdered, maimed, or incarcerated. The Shark would lose his leg in a car bombing. Chicken Man Testa was blown up. Little Nicky Scarfo went to prison for murder. Angelo "the Docile Don" Bruno was shot in his car. Frank "the Irishman" Sheeran received a thirty-two-year prison sentence but eventually died in a nursing home. Russell "McGee" Bufalino was sentenced to ten years for plotting a murder but died a free man. Sam "Momo"

Vito Genovese wanted to be "boss of bosses." His ruthless and ambitious methods led to the exposure of a vast secret network of organized crime.
[Library of Congress]

Giancana was killed by gunshot while cooking sausages in his kitchen. Some victims were killed while eating in a restaurant or walking down the street. Others were found buried in concrete or rumored to be in the trunk of a car that had been melted down at a wrecking yard. Some victims disappeared so completely that the bodies were never found.

They used harmless-sounding phrases to convey violent intent.

"I heard you paint houses" referred to murder and leaving blood on the walls. Telling a man "what it is" or kissing him on the mouth was as good as a death threat. "I do my own carpentry work" meant the person got rid of bodies. "Don't bring a piece; it's a muscle job" meant no guns—someone is going to get beat up.

JIMMY AND THE MOB

As Jimmy worked to get new members into the union, he learned to protect himself from employers, police, goon squads, the Mafia, and any enemies that he made along the way. But sometimes he worked with members of the mob. He also had his own cruel ways to do business or had others do it for him. For instance, a man who had a radio show that featured anti-Hoffa Teamsters was blinded when acid was thrown into his face as he left a restaurant.

In the wake of the Apalachin raid, J. Edgar Hoover, director of the FBI, created the Top Hoodlum Program, and the FBI began investigating members of the Mafia. In 1961, U.S. Attorney General Robert Kennedy, brother of President John F. Kennedy, put greater emphasis and Justice Department lawyers on those investigations. Robert Kennedy had previously been chief counsel to the Senate's Select Committee on Improper Activities in the Labor and Management Field. With his new role, he was more determined than ever to stop Jimmy Hoffa and his corrupt activities. He eventually had many

Caesars Palace in Las Vegas, Nevada, was financed in part with a $10.6 million loan from the Teamsters pension fund. [Library of Congress]

attorneys and FBI agents working for him on his Get Hoffa squad, and grand juries in thirteen states heard testimony against Jimmy and his associates. The federal investigators used spies and wiretapping, but for years they could not get a conviction. Sometimes the government did not have a very good case. At other times Jimmy or his supporters may have bullied or bribed a witness or a juror.

During the Senate committee hearing, when Kennedy or his team questioned any witness associated with Jimmy, the person on the stand used the Fifth Amendment of the Constitution to respond: "Senator, on advice of counsel, I respectfully decline to answer that question on the grounds that it might tend to incriminate me." This is called pleading the Fifth.

Union rules prevented Jimmy from using this response or he would forfeit his job. Therefore he used a lot of doubletalk. He might say, "I don't remember." Sometimes he would say that he didn't remember and to ask someone else, and that person would then plead the Fifth.

But more typical recorded answers would be like these: "To the best of my recollection, I must recall on my memory, I cannot remember." Or "I can say here to the Chair that I cannot recall in answer to your question other than to say I just don't recall my recollection."

One day in a Nashville courtroom, a man rushed in and shot Jimmy in the back. Jimmy turned and decked him. Jimmy had bruises on his back but was not seriously injured. The man had brought a BB gun usually used for squirrels and rabbits.

U.S. Attorney General Robert Kennedy testifying before a Senate committee hearing on crime. [Library of Congress]

There were several investigations and trials that ended with no convictions, but Robert Kennedy was relentless. Jimmy was finally found guilty on charges of jury tampering, conspiracy, and fraud

Jimmy (right) consulted with Bernard Spindel, a professional wiretapper, as they pleaded not guilty to illegal wiretap charges. [Library of Congress]

relating to the Teamsters pension fund and sentenced to thirteen years in prison. Jimmy fought the convictions for three years but lost his appeals. He went into the federal penitentiary at Lewisburg, Pennsylvania, on March 7, 1967, and became inmate 33298NE.

He named Frank Fitzsimmons, his right-hand man, to run the

union in his absence. He later wrote that he had made two big mistakes in his life. The first was getting involved in what he called a "blood feud" with Robert Kennedy. The second was turning everything over to Frank Fitzsimmons.

JIMMY IN PRISON

As a prisoner, Hoffa did not stop being an organizer for better conditions. He wrote up a list of nineteen grievances for the prison warden, trying to improve the food, medical care, and dental care for the inmates, who he felt were being treated "like wild animals." He talked with congressmen and anyone who would listen about his efforts and did get assurances for food without grubs and twenty-four-hour medical care for the inmates. After his release, Hoffa would continue working for inmates with the National Association for Justice, a privately funded prison reform group. Later, when he wrote a book, the proceeds went to this organization.

A "Free Hoffa" movement was started with bumper stickers, buttons, and patches. Every year a plane flew over the prison dragging a birthday greeting for Jimmy. Every Christmas, Jimmy got thousands of cards from Teamsters supporters. A petition filled with 250,000 signatures was submitted for his release.

Inmates old and new asked to talk with Jimmy. They wanted real jobs when they got out, but they received no job training while in prison. They were only allowed to make license plates and mop buckets, which were not skills that they could use on the outside. Jimmy helped many of them.

POWERFUL ENEMIES

One person he did not help was Anthony "Tony Pro" Provenzano, who ran the Teamsters local in northern New Jersey and was a captain in the Genovese crime family in New York. He was in the same prison with Jimmy. Jimmy was going to get a $1.7 million pension from the Central States Pension Fund, but Tony Pro was in prison for extortion and had lost his pension. Teamsters rules took away a pension from those convicted of extortion.

Tony Pro asked for help, but Jimmy refused. "It's because of people like you," he reportedly said, "that I got into trouble in the first place."

Tony Pro was very angry about this, and Jimmy added another powerful person to his list of enemies. This mobster was ruthless and would later be convicted for ordering the murder of a union rival.

On December 23, 1971, after fifty-eight months in prison, Jimmy's sentence was commuted by President Richard M. Nixon. However, a condition was attached to his release. He was not allowed to participate in union activities until 1980. Jimmy fought this, saying the restriction was not on the conditions-of-release form he had signed in prison. He wanted to run for president of his old Detroit Local 299 and eventually challenge Frank Fitzsimmons for control of the national union. Jimmy withdrew from the race when federal officials said he would risk going back to prison.

While Jimmy was held at Lewisburg, Frank Fitzsimmons decided he liked being union president and didn't want to give it up. Jimmy thought Fitzsimmons had teamed up with Nixon to block his return. "No one has ever been disloyal like this rat Fitz," Jimmy growled.

Fitzsimmons had done a poor job in negotiating good deals for the Teamsters. He had also been making huge loans to the Mafia from the pension fund, which now had assets over $1.2 billion. The loans were not getting repaid.

When Jimmy was released and talked about a return to leadership, he said he was going to clean up the union. He intended to get the loans repaid and expose the mob connections. Jimmy had many backers in the Teamsters organization. The majority of its officers and members were honest and hardworking, and they enjoyed one of the highest standards of living of any union in the country. Jimmy was not supposed to get in touch with his old labor pals, but he did travel around the country for the National Association of Justice. In this way he was able to meet with supporters without looking like he was doing any union business.

As Jimmy worked to get back to a position of power, he let it be known that he had records and lists that would be mailed off to the FBI if anything happened to him. Tony Pro, the New Jersey Teamster with ties to the mob, threatened Jimmy's granddaughter, and mob boss Russell Bufalino put out the message, "Tell him what it is."

On July 30, 1975, Jimmy thought he had a 2:00 p.m. meeting with Detroit mobster Anthony "Tony Jack" Giacalone and Tony Pro. They were to meet at the Machus Red Fox Restaurant outside Detroit.

Jimmy stopped on the way to talk with a friend and mentioned the meeting. When he arrived at the restaurant, no one was there.

Jimmy waited until 2:30 p.m. but no one showed up. He walked to a phone booth and called his wife. She hadn't heard from anyone, and Jimmy said he'd be home by four. About 2:45 p.m. Jimmy was seen getting into another car. Witnesses had conflicting details about the vehicle and who was in it.

The car drove off, and no one heard from Jimmy again. Ever.

James Riddle Hoffa disappeared.

ALIBIS AND THEORIES

Jimmy's car was found unlocked at the restaurant with no clues inside.

Tony Pro had an alibi. He was in New Jersey playing Greek rummy. Tony Jack had an alibi, too. He was getting a massage at a health club in Detroit. Both denied that they had arranged a meeting.

The FBI put two hundred agents on the disappearance and eventually accumulated seventy volumes of files (sixteen thousand pages) called the Hoffex file. They had nine suspects who appeared before a grand jury. All pleaded the Fifth. Immunity was offered for information, but no one took it.

Over the years, many stories and theories about Jimmy's disappearance have surfaced.

Anthony Zerilli, a Detroit mobster, told New York's NBC 4 that Hoffa was buried in a Michigan field about twenty miles north of the restaurant.

Ralph Picardo, an FBI Teamsters informant, said Jimmy's body was put in a fifty-five-gallon steel drum and carted away in a truck. He didn't know where it was taken, but one theory was that it ended up at a toxic-waste site in Jersey City, New Jersey.

Donald "Tony the Greek" Frankos claimed that Jimmy's body was taken to New Jersey, mixed into concrete, and buried in the end zone of the New York Giants' football stadium. Officials with body-detection equipment never found anything. Later, when Giants Stadium was torn down, another search was made, with the same negative results.

A contract killer named Charles Allen told Senate investigators that Tony Pro had told him Jimmy was "ground up in little pieces, shipped to Florida and thrown into a swamp."

Another theory was that he was buried at the Sheraton Savannah Resort in Georgia, owned by the Teamsters at the time.

Or buried in a gravel pit in Highland, Michigan, owned by Jimmy's brother, Billy?

Or crushed in an automobile compactor at a sanitation company in Michigan?

Another contract killer, Richard "the Big Guy" Kuklinski, had his own story. He said Tony Pro engaged him and two brothers to go after "a union guy" in Detroit. The "mark" had to disappear "forever." Tony Pro was in the car, contrary to his alibi, when Kuklinski killed the mark with a knife. They put the body in a bag in the trunk, and Kuklinski drove all the way to a junkyard in New Jersey under the Pulaski Skyway. The body ended up in a black fifty-gallon drum and was set on fire. The drum was then welded shut and buried in the junkyard. The pay for this was $40,000.

Later, when one of the brothers started talking to federal investigators, "the drum was quickly dug up and placed in the trunk of a car that was smashed down to a four-by-two-foot cube of metal in a giant car compressor. It, along with hundreds of other compacted cars, was then sold to the Japanese as scrap metal and shipped off to Japan to be used in the making of new automobiles that would compete with Detroit carmakers' products. That's what happened to Teamsters Union boss Jimmy Hoffa."

Frank "the Irishman" Sheeran confessed on his deathbed that he killed Hoffa, according to author Charles Brandt. Sheeran said that he was Jimmy's best friend and that because he was present, Jimmy got into a different car at the restaurant. Then they drove to a nearby house, where Jimmy was killed. Frank said that if he hadn't agreed to kill Jimmy, then he himself would have been killed. The floorboards of the house he identified were pulled up. Blood was found, but of twenty-eight possible samples, DNA was found on only two. The DNA was compared to a sample of Jimmy's hair, but the results were inconclusive, according to the FBI lab report.

No body, blood, or DNA samples have been found to validate any of these theories.

Hoffa was declared legally dead in 1982. The FBI Hoffex file was turned over to the Michigan state attorney. That file has been closed but is available to read online.

Jimmy's son, James P. Hoffa, has been general president of the International Brotherhood of Teamsters since 1999.

Safeguards were set up in the 1980s to protect the Central States Pension Fund. However, the fund is running out of money. This is due to a reduction in the number of trucking companies paying into the fund to cover their employees and a smaller union workforce overall. Now older union members are retiring in record numbers, and there are fewer truckers to keep the account funded. The federal government has barred Central States from cutting the retirement benefits of its 407,000 participants. The pension currently pays out $3.46 for every $1 paid into the fund. If the math continues, the pension fund will eventually be drained for lack of participation.

If Jimmy is in a grave somewhere, he might be rolling over.

CHAPTER 2

D. B. Cooper, Down, Down, Down, and Gone

With your pleasant smile
And your dropout style,
D. B. Cooper, where did you go?
—from Judy Sword's folk ballad "D. B. Cooper, Where Are You?"

A ONE-WAY TICKET

ON THANKSGIVING EVE, November 24, 1971, a man wearing a dark suit, a white shirt, a black clip-on tie, and an overcoat entered the airport in Portland, Oregon. Carrying a briefcase, he looked like any ordinary businessman as he paid $20 cash for a one-way ticket on Northwest Orient Airlines Flight 305 to Seattle. He gave his name as Dan Cooper.

The plane he boarded was a Boeing 727. This jet was a popular model around the world because it could land in areas with short runways or even no runways at all. The 727 was also unusual because it had a staircase under its tail, called an aft airstairs, which could be opened during flight. In addition, its three engines were mounted high, allowing someone to jump from the stairs and not be injured by jet exhaust.

Not many people knew about these features, but Cooper did. He had done his homework. This was just the plane he wanted to board.

Cooper chose a seat in the very last row by the lavatory, where the aisle, middle, and window seats were vacant. A college student reading a book sat across the aisle from him. It was a quiet pre-holiday flight with thirty-six passengers on a plane that could hold eighty-nine. With open seating, most of the passengers sat up front. Could

D. B. Cooper diving in a free fall from Northwest Orient Airlines Flight 305.

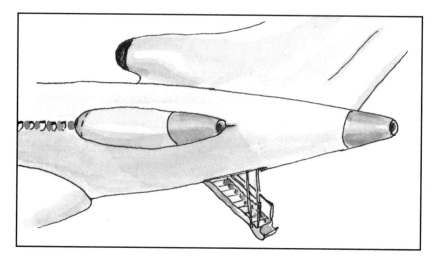

The Boeing 727 aft airstairs. A person with a military background would be more likely to know that something, or someone, could drop from these stairs while in flight.

this be just as he wanted it? No one around to ask personal questions?

Cooper ordered a bourbon and 7Up and lit one cigarette after another. He smoked Raleigh filter tips, an inexpensive brand that could be bought with coupons.

BETTER READ THAT NOTE!

The plane got ready for the thirty-six-minute hop to Seattle. Already it was getting dark, and the night would be even darker, as there would be no moon. Cooper called to flight attendant Florence Schaffner and gave her an envelope. Flo was young and pretty and often got notes from passengers. Busy with other work, she slipped the paper into her pocket, but the man kept looking at her and nodding.

She opened the note and asked if he was kidding. "No, miss," he said. "This is for real." The note revealed that he was a hijacker. "I have a bomb here and I would like you to sit by me." When she sat, he flipped open the briefcase to reveal wires, a battery, and red-colored cylinders bundled together.

Flight attendant Tina Mucklow read the note also. Cooper dictated another note and Flo took it to the pilot, Captain William Scott. He was in the cockpit with copilot Bill Rataczak and flight engineer Harold Anderson. Cooper's note demanded two back parachutes, two front parachutes, and $200,000 in used bills inside a knapsack. He also wanted a service truck ready to refuel the jet in Seattle.

Cooper told Captain Scott to circle the Seattle airport until all the hijacking demands were met. He and Tina talked to the cockpit through the interphone. Because the "black box" recorder for the interphone self-erased every thirty minutes, Flo stayed up front and took notes on everything that Cooper said.

Captain Scott called airline officials, and the president of Northwest Orient instructed the crew to meet Cooper's demands. In the early days of air piracy, there was little screening of passengers. Most hijackers wanted to go to Cuba, but this was different. The airline president thought giving in would be the best way to keep everyone safe. The airline also had insurance to cover most of the $200,000. In 2017, this amount would be worth about $1.2 million.

The crew on Flight 305 managed to remain calm. The college student sitting nearby did not notice anything unusual but was unhappy with the lack of attention from the flight attendant.

THE RUSH TO MEET DEMANDS

While the 727 circled over Puget Sound, frantic efforts were made by FBI officials to borrow money from a Seattle bank before the plane ran out of fuel. They managed to get stacks of used twenties issued in San Francisco.

Quickly the bills were photographed with a high-speed machine called a Recordak, and the images with the serial numbers were stored on microfilm. Later this information would be sent to banks and businesses across the country. But on this harried night they hustled to bind the stacks of money with paper tape and pack them into a canvas bag. Then it was a race to get it to the airport as soon as possible.

The search for parachutes was even more frenzied. The FBI suggested getting some from nearby McChord Air Force Base. Cooper was aware of the local geography and thought it should take only twenty minutes to get the chutes from there. Was he really planning to jump? Was he hoping that no one would be able to spot a man in dark clothes dropping through the blackness of night? At the last minute he could pull the rip cord. Only then would a colorful canopy balloon out to slow him for a soft landing.

After inquiries at several places, authorities contacted Linn Emrich from a local skydiving center. He was able to locate two chest packs

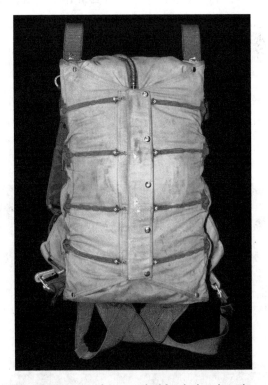

One of the four parachutes packed for the hijacker. This one was left on the plane and held for evidence by the FBI.
[2013.35.1, Washington State Historical Society, Tacoma (Wash.)]

with no rip cords. The two backpacks that did have them were provided by local pilot Norman Hayden. With sirens screaming, state troopers raced to Seattle-Tacoma Airport so the plane, still circling and running low on fuel, could finally land.

On the tarmac Cooper released all thirty-six passengers in exchange for the parachutes and cash. While the plane was refueling, the pilot was told to set the heading for Mexico City. Cooper wanted the aft airstairs extended for takeoff. Fly slow, he demanded. No lights in the cabin. Keep the landing wheels down. Extend the wing flaps fifteen degrees. He also insisted that the plane not exceed ten thousand feet in elevation. Below this altitude, the plane would not have to be pressurized with oxygen. It was also an altitude high enough to allow a free fall for thousands of feet.

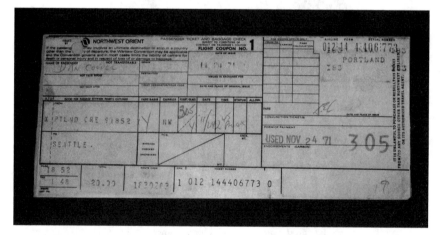

D. B. Cooper's plane ticket. [FBI]

How did Cooper know so much about how to fly the Boeing 727? What did he have in mind as he insisted on specific flight details?

The cockpit informed him that takeoff with the stairs extended was impossible and warned that the method of flying would burn through jet fuel too rapidly to make it to Mexico City. Cooper agreed that the stairs could be extended after takeoff and that the plane could go to Reno, Nevada. The pilot followed a low-altitude course between the interstate freeway and the Cascade Mountains called Victor 23.

All the flight requirements contributed to confusion about Cooper's possible plan. Why keep the airstairs down? Why fly so low? Was he going to use the parachutes or not? Maybe he wanted to force someone else to jump? If anyone jumped, could the person even survive on such a cold, windy, moonless night?

DISAPPEARING INTO THE NIGHT

Only the pilot, copilot, flight engineer, and flight attendant Tina Mucklow remained aboard when the plane departed from Sea-Tac. Tina stayed in the back with Cooper, who was upset because the money had been delivered in a bag. He had wanted a knapsack with a zipper and handles. He cut open a parachute with a salmon-pink canopy and removed the nylon cords. He used these to wrap the money sack into a two-foot bundle.

Cooper asked how to open the airstairs. The cockpit advised Tina to tie herself up so she wouldn't be sucked outside. Cooper, however, told her to go to the cockpit and stay there with the rest of the crew. He would extend the stairs himself. When she last saw him, he was in the aisle with a nylon cord tied around his waist.

The crew in the cockpit was behind a closed door with no window. They were unable to monitor Cooper's activities. For a while they had contact over the interphone. At Cooper's request, the pilot leveled off and reduced the speed. The copilot asked if there was anything else they could do for him. "No," came the response. Then all was quiet.

Meanwhile, two F-106 fighter aircraft from McChord Air Force Base were up in the air trying to follow the dragging Boeing 727. These streamlined jets were not built to fly slowly and had to zigzag back and forth, back and forth, looking for the unlit hijacked plane. Even with radar, the pilots couldn't find it. They kept their eyes glued to the window with hopes of spotting a puffed-up parachute as it drifted below. But on this cloudy, moonless night they were called back to base without ever seeing the 727 or a parachuting hijacker.

Back at Sea-Tac Airport, a roll call of passengers revealed that Dan Cooper was the only one to stay on the plane. He was the hijacker. The others did not yet know about the situation, and some were unhappy that the plane had been behind schedule.

As the passengers got more information, they were asked for witness descriptions of Cooper. Their answers were mixed. His suit was

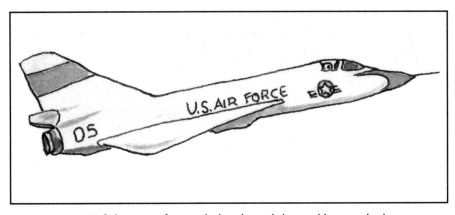

F-106 fighter aircraft were sleek and speedy but could not go slowly.
They had to zigzag back and forth behind the hijacked plane.

brown. No, it was black? No, russet? He had short, greased black hair? No, he had brown hair. An olive complexion? Midforties? Loafers? No, sturdy shoes.

Flo saw him without sunglasses and said his eyes were brown. Both Flo and Tina would give very similar descriptions of Cooper. Tina, who spent the most time with him, said he was usually polite.

Shortly after the hijacking, the FBI used this information to create a WANTED bulletin. They were looking for a white male in his midforties, five feet ten inches to six feet tall. He had an olive complexion, dark brown or black hair parted on the left and combed back, possibly brown eyes. Two composite sketches were made of him, one with sunglasses and one without, and the bulletin was sent out everywhere.

A RED LIGHT AND A SHUDDER

Around 8:00 p.m. the crew in the cockpit of the 727 noticed a red light. This indicated the rear stairs had been lowered. Soon they felt a shudder. The captain described it as a "curtsy," where the nose tipped up and then down. The crew stayed in the cockpit as instructed. They were flying over the majestic cedar, fir, and hemlock forests of the Pacific Northwest. It was also an area where stories of Bigfoot, also known as Sasquatch, had become part of the folklore.

When the plane reached Oregon, FBI agent Ralph Himmelsbach, a former World War II fighter pilot, went up in a helicopter with two National Guard pilots. They were unable to find the 727 and returned to the Portland airport. Then a Lockheed T-33 of the Air National Guard was able to fly slowly and spot the plane. It followed the Boeing 727 down to Klamath Falls, Oregon, and then ran low on fuel. It never spotted a parachutist.

The Northwest Orient flight took a left turn and finally landed in Reno at 10:15 p.m. The FBI, Federal Aviation Administration, local police, airport security, and an army unit were all waiting for it. As the jet screeched by, they watched the dangling airstairs scrape the tarmac and throw off sparks. Then they raced after the plane and tried to see if the hijacker might leap from the airstairs and escape into the darkness. They saw nothing.

Suspect sketches created by the FBI. [FBI]

Once safely on the ground, Captain Scott called the hijacker. There was no response. The crew opened the door, pushed past the first-class curtain, and looked into the cabin. Empty. Agents rushed onboard to find a good parachute, the opened salmon-pink parachute, a thin black clip-on tie, a ticket, the remains of eight cigarettes, and four plastic drinking glasses. Over many years this material was checked and rechecked for fingerprints and DNA, but none of it led to the identity of the hijacker.

Cooper, the money, and two parachutes were gone. The hijacker took a rip-cord backpack parachute and a chest pack dummy that was not functional. Apparently, in the rush to meet Cooper's demands, the dummy instructional parachute had been grabbed by mistake.

But had Cooper known the chute was nonfunctional? If so, why would he take that one and leave a better one behind? Had he really jumped, or did he throw the parachutes out to cause confusion and then sneak off the plane in Reno? Could he be injured? Had he even survived? And where, oh where, was all that money?

As one police officer later said, "Would *you* bail out of a plane at night if you could think of a better way?"

At this point there was only one thing they knew for certain.

Somewhere between Seattle and Reno, Cooper simply disappeared.

LOOKING FOR D. B. COOPER

The world was intrigued by this air piracy because it was like nothing ever seen before. Almost from the very first moment, Cooper was becoming a legend.

Did he really jump? The shudder in the plane led the FBI to conduct an experiment to see what it meant. They used the same plane and pilot and an experienced parachuter. The results indicated that Cooper really had jumped. They estimated the time between 8:11 p.m. and 8:16 p.m., and this narrowed the drop zone to somewhere near Ariel, Washington, and Lake Merwin. This was a big area, covering about twenty-five square miles.

It didn't take long for entrepreneurs to start selling T-shirts and hats. Some wrote songs and books. Cooper quickly gained notoriety as someone who had jumped from a windy airstairs, clutching a large amount of money and floating through the blackness to "somewhere." Maybe he'd plopped into deep Lake Merwin? Maybe he was dangling from the top of a tree? Maybe he was dead? Or maybe, just maybe, he had drifted down, down, down, folded up the parachute, and walked away with a bundle of riches.

In the confusion of trying to get more details, a reporter was told the hijacker was named D. Cooper. He heard it wrong and reported the suspect as D. B. Cooper. These initials were passed along in the

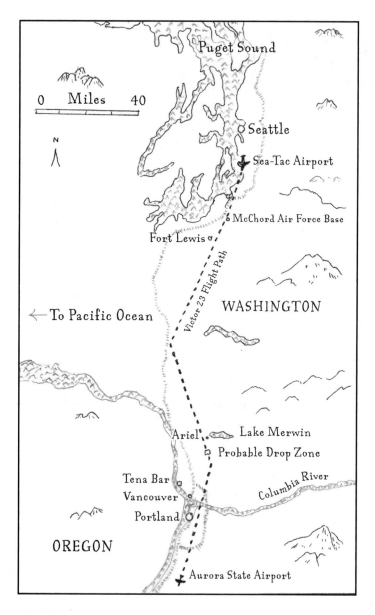

Map of flight and estimated drop zone.

news media and not corrected by the FBI for a year. The agents thought this would help them sort out the clues that would surely come in. Anyone claiming to be D. B. would not realize that the real hijacker used the name Dan.

Meanwhile, search teams were looking everywhere in the drop zone, on the ground and from the air. Helicopters checked the slopes for a parachute dangling in the trees. Agents knocked on doors and stopped cars. Reporters investigated, amateurs scoured the area, and even airline workers were involved. The November weather was cloudy and cold, which made the search difficult. Northwest offered a reward of $25,000 for information, and the *Seattle Post-Intelligencer* newspaper offered $5,000.

GATHERING CLUES

The FBI considered the parachutes given to Cooper. One was an old military parachute that would be very hard to steer. One was a Pioneer brand with padded arm and leg straps. Was Cooper's choice of the military parachute important? Did he have a military background? Later they wondered why he took the dummy chute, which was sewn shut. Didn't he recognize what it was? Maybe he didn't know as much about parachuting as they originally thought.

Many D. B. Coopers and their relatives across the country were questioned. For instance, one Cooper named Darryl said his parents and aunts and uncles were all approached. When the FBI came knocking at the door, Darryl's father asked, "Who put you up to this?" The family did a lot of joking, and the father thought this was yet another effort to get a laugh. The federal agents flashed their badges and continued with no-nonsense demands to get answers. Finally the father realized the questions were serious and cooperated. The FBI went on to interview Darryl's employer. They were able to provide an alibi because Darryl was on a business trip for them at the time of the hijacking. He was flying under the name on his business cards, D. B. Cooper. The FBI never questioned Darryl himself after confirming this alibi.

Many people did not believe that Cooper could have survived. Or if he did, he must have been injured. They checked hospitals, clinics, and pharmacies but came up with no useful information.

After weeks of searching, snow covered the area, and they had to wait until it melted in the spring of 1972. Then more agents and two hundred soldiers thoroughly combed through the search zone again. This time a body was found, but it was not D. B. Cooper. No piece of a parachute, not even a thread, was ever discovered.

COPYCATS AND IMITATORS

In April 1972, there was a copycat hijacking. A man named Richard McCoy boarded a Boeing 727 in Denver and then ordered the pilot to fly to San Francisco. He demanded $500,000 and four parachutes. He had a pistol, a grenade, and his own jumpsuit. After D. B. Cooper's jump, Boeing began drilling little peepholes in the cockpit doors of their 727s. They also added the "Cooper vane," or "Dan Cooper switch," a hinged outside plate that is pushed against the airstairs by airflow and prevents them from being opened in flight. On this plane the airstairs had not yet been modified, but a fish-eye peephole had been added. McCoy covered it with tape.

"Dan Cooper switch." Airflow from a moving airplane shifts a plate on the aft airstairs to keep them from opening while in flight.

When the plane took off, McCoy parachuted from the open aft airstairs over Utah. Police were able to catch him in two days, thanks to a tip from a neighbor and handwriting analysis of one of his notes to the cockpit. The money was found in his house, and McCoy was convicted and sentenced to forty-five years in prison. Two years later he escaped with three other inmates using a fake gun carved out of dental wax and drove away in a garbage truck. FBI agents found him in Virginia Beach, Virginia, where he was killed in a shootout.

Some people thought then, and some still do, that McCoy was the real Cooper and not an imitator. However, he was only twenty-nine, and Cooper was remembered as being much older. Also, McCoy was wearing a dark curly wig and makeup to darken his skin. The FBI eventually discovered that McCoy had been in Las Vegas on the day of the hijacking, and the McCoy family gave him an alibi. He spent Thanksgiving Day with his family in Utah.

In 1972 alone, there were fifteen Cooper-like airplane hijackings demanding parachutes. The airports installed better screening, and the FBI caught all the perpetrators. But the real D. B. Cooper remained elusive.

Another suspect was Kenneth Christiansen, who had trained as an army paratrooper. His younger brother was convinced Kenneth was D. B. Cooper and wrote to the FBI. Kenneth died in 1994, at the age of sixty-seven. On his deathbed Kenneth said, "There is something you should know, but I cannot tell you!" Kenneth did have a large, unexplained amount of money. However, the FBI was able to rule him out because he had the wrong body size and eye color.

Robert Rackstraw, a Vietnam veteran, has been investigated for many years. In 2018, he resurfaced in the news, possibly tied to a coded message that some consider a disguised confession. A photo of Rackstraw was shown to Tina Mucklow, who said she "did not find any similarities."

D. B. Cooper always attracted a lot of attention. The agents in charge of the case were contacted by police from many jurisdictions. They also heard from serious clue seekers, crackpots, clairvoyants, treasure hunters, and publicity hounds. Many people were investigated. Many confessed. Numerous theories were developed, books written, T-shirts sold, and ballads sung. The legendary status of D. B. Cooper kept growing.

A party for the hijacker was started in 1974 at the Ariel General Store and Tavern in Ariel, Washington, on the Saturday after Thanksgiving. Hundreds would gather and sing songs and eat buffalo stew each year in his honor. Some came wearing sunglasses and a parachute and carrying a bag of money. They bought T-shirts printed with D. B. COOPER FAN CLUB and COOPER LIVES!

People are still out investigating various new leads about his identity. They hope that crew members of the hijacked jet will look at just one more picture and say, "That's him. I'm sure that's him." But so far those words have not been spoken.

Eventually a clue came from a comic book called *Dan Cooper*. Agents wondered if this could be the source of his name. The comic-book Cooper was a test pilot in the Royal Canadian Air Force who would parachute out of planes. Since the series was published in Belgium and written in French, maybe the hijacker had visited Europe? Or maybe he was from Canada? Investigating these possibilities did not help uncover Cooper's real identity.

As always, D. B. Cooper remained a mystery that no one could solve.

MONEY ON A SANDBAR

Finally, after eight years of dead ends, a real, we-can-hold-it-in-our-hands clue was found. In 1980, the Ingram family was visiting Tena Bar, a sandbar on the Washington State side of the Columbia River. Eight-year-old Brian Ingram, a third grader, was smoothing out bumpy sand so that his father could build a fire. The bump turned out to be three rotting packets of money—290 twenty-dollar bills, adding up to $5,800. It was a huge sum for this family, who had recently moved from Oklahoma.

The Ingrams turned it in, and the FBI checked it out. The money was dirty and worn and wrapped in rubber bands. But the serial numbers were readable, and they turned up on the list of money given

Some of the money found by eight-year-old Brian Ingram. [FBI]

to Cooper! Finally they had something tangible to study. Would it solve the case?

Cooper's flight had followed a path several miles to the east. Tena Bar was eighteen miles as the crow flies south of Cooper's drop zone. There was no stream out of the area that could have carried the money to the sandbar. How did it get there? And when?

The bar had been dredged in 1974 to clear a channel in the river. Huge machines had dug sand from the river bottom and dumped it on the bar. Then they added a layer of clay. Since the packets were

Brian Ingram at age fourteen, after winning back a portion of the Cooper bills.

[Michael Lloyd, *The Oregonian*]

found on the top layer, wouldn't they have to have been there after 1974?

Another problem was the rubber bands. They don't last long out in nature, so the money had to arrive on the bar within the recent past. Someone must have hidden the money there not too long before Brian found it, maybe in 1979 or 1980? But who? And why? A complete study of the sand, the clay, and the currents revealed no trace of the remainder of the $200,000.

Brian's lucky find raised more new questions that could not be answered. The rest of the money has never turned up anywhere, so if Cooper survived, he may have lost it or felt unsafe spending it. The search area was later redirected to the Washougal River drainage area, but this new focus has never turned up anything useful, either.

The investigators put the tattered money into an evidence safe so it could be used to prosecute Cooper if he was ever identified. Several years earlier, an indictment had been made against Cooper, or whatever his name might turn out to be, so that if Cooper was ever captured, he could still be brought to trial. Otherwise the time allowed for prosecutors to charge him with the hijacking would run out.

Northwest Airlines rewarded Brian with $500, and the *Oregon Journal* gave him $250. The much larger awards were no longer available. Brian became the only person to receive a reward of any kind. Some of the money was eventually returned to him. He sold a portion of it to collectors for $37,433.

The J. C. Penney necktie left behind. [FBI]

For over forty-five years this mystery has remained as the only un-solved case of air piracy in U.S. history. Between 1971 and 2016, the FBI investigated over twelve hundred serious suspects. They also took a look at the hundreds and hundreds more who confessed to being D. B Cooper. For many reasons people wanted to be a part of this story, which kept getting more fantastic and legendary as time went by.

The FBI simply couldn't solve it. The bureau finally closed the case on July 11, 2016, and moved stacks of evidence from Seattle to Washington, D.C., for historical storage.

The bureau did, however, give a small scientific team permission to search the crime vault for evidence. Using an electron microscope that can find particles the size of a human blood cell, the team was able to study more than a hundred thousand particles on the tie that couldn't be seen before. They discovered pure titanium and other metals such as cerium, yttrium, and aluminum. In the 1970s, Boeing used a titanium alloy, but a parts supplier in Oregon may have used pure titanium. The team has been appealing to anyone who might have knowledge of an unhappy worker—maybe someone in a chemical plant or metal fabrication plant who simply did not show up for work after the hijacking.

The FBI might reopen the case for a solid clue like a parachute, a body, or any of the 9,710 bills that are still missing. Without something to hold in their hands, there may never be an answer to this often-asked question:

"D. B. Cooper, where are you?"

CHAPTER 3

Barbara Follett, a Child Author

It is Eepersip, The House Without Windows, my story,
my story in New York, with the Knopfs,
to be published!! . . . PUBLISHED!!!!!!!
—Barbara Follett, age twelve, referring to her story of
over 40,000 words that she originally wrote at age eight

LETTERS, NUMBERS, AND COMMAS, TOO

BARBARA NEWHALL FOLLETT was born in Hanover, New Hampshire, on March 4, 1914. Her parents were writers, editors, readers, and instructors—prominent in the creative world of language and literature. This child was surrounded with words.

When she was five months old, her father, Wilson Follett, wrote, "I hang on the queer motions of your hands; my spirit dissolves in ecstasies over the inscrutable things you do with your dimpled feet; I marvel over your limpid baby-eyes that grow browner and browner; and everlastingly I speculate about what you mean by all these things."

Two months later her mother, Helen, wrote that Barbara's favorite playthings were strings. She would roll and tumble "in a wondrous fashion." She made "the discovery of producing a noise by hitting two things together . . . and delighting us all with your whackings."

It is not unusual for babies to have dimples or to create a delightful method for moving around. But as Barbara grew, unlike most toddlers, she quickly and thoroughly became interested in letters and numbers. She imitated her grandmother Ding and learned to count to

Barbara at her typewriter.

Barbara reading with her father in the fall of 1916.

ten. Over and over she put her finger on a letter and asked what it was. For a brief period of time she confused a *V* with an *A*.

Then on January 16, 1916, Helen recorded, "Today *she knows every letter in the alphabet.*" Barbara was just twenty-two months old.

Books had now become Barbara's passion, and she knew all the nursery rhymes. She was also intrigued by two unusual volumes: *A Grammar for Thinkers* and the catalog for Harvard College. Her mother wrote that this fascination "comes from her love for commas and periods! (Ridiculous!)"

Soon Barbara started compressing long words into something shorter. *Handkerchief* became *hank*. *Bottle* became *bot*. *Potato* became *tate*. She saw letters everywhere, in books and on boards and signs. Helen wrote that she "even sees them where they don't exist, as for example—in certain accumulations of dust on the ceiling!"

As Barbara turned three, she began to read simple words like *rain*, *ring*, and *some*. Within three days she added harder words: *protect*, *disturb*, *muddy*. She also began to make up words. For instance, a toothbrush became a butterfly brush because she could make it splash on the wall to look like butter flying.

TAP, TAP, TAP ON THE TYPEWRITER

In September 1917, when Barbara was three and a half, she became intrigued with the Corona typewriter in the house. This was a great

At the age of three and a half, Barbara began learning how to use a typewriter. [Library of Congress]

discovery for a budding writer because she was too young to hold a pencil well, but a typewriter suited her perfectly.

Soon Barbara knew how to roll in the paper, use the space bar, and push the carriage back when the bell rang. She typed the same words over and over: *to, come, away, bluebird.* She was reading well enough to get through the Aldine Readers, a series of primers usually used by older children. She learned to count to one hundred and could add and subtract. She also created her first poem.

Motor, motor come along

Linger, binger, dinger dong

When Barbara was four, she typed her first letter, including capitals and commas. Her mother helped with the spelling.

March 16, 1918
Dear Cousin Helen:
I love the birds. I love the dish, and I love
the card. I pasted the little birds into the
little book all alone, but 'cept the first
one Mother did. The birds were broken, but
Mother mended them with glue. Thank you very
much.
Barbara Newhall Follett

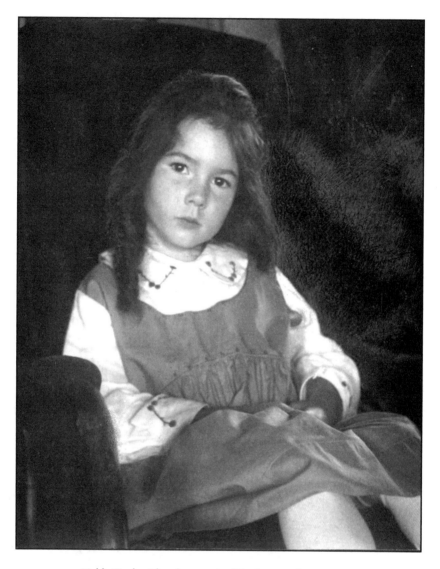

Holdo Teodor Oberg's portrait of Barbara at about age six.

[Barbara Newhall Follett papers, Columbia University Libraries]

In 1919, Helen decided to homeschool her daughter with a big emphasis on using the typewriter. One assignment was to write letters. Barbara began writing to several people, including Holdo Teodor Oberg, a Swedish immigrant with an antiques-restoration shop. His collection of ticking clocks became Barbara's new favorite thing. The two of them also shared a love of nature. Mr. Oberg sent her many gifts and kept in good repair some things she owned, like her stuffed rabbit.

"Thank you for the little picture of the roosters and rabbits," Barbara wrote in one letter. Then another time: "The goldfinches come every afternoon and eat their supper on the clump of bachelor's-buttons right on the left-hand side of the path." Throughout her childhood, she would exchange letters with relatives and many other people she met. These included writers of children's books, scientists, and several sailors and captains of ships. Some she met at Lake Sunapee in New Hampshire, her favorite place to spend a summer vacation.

She shared her love of the outdoors with naturalist Edward Porter St. John, dean of the Auburn Theological Seminary in upstate New York. "Just then I made a discovery—some small blue flowers, liverwort, which I later found were the same as the hepatica which you mentioned. . . . Wood anemones peeped at me from behind the logs and the trees behind us, peeping like little gnomes and fairies; up a tiny trickle of a brook marched stately yellow adder's tongue. . . . On the shores of another brook were skunk cabbages; the liverwort was scattered in symphonies of color."

When she was six and a half, Barbara wrote a story with four chapters. It was thirteen pages long and titled "The Life of the Spinning-Wheel, the Rocking-Horse, and the Rabbit." Later she wrote to Mr. Oberg, asking if he had read it. "Well, I am beginning a new adventure of how they got traveling to China. If you come to see me I will read it to you." The sequel had sixteen pages.

MUSIC AND DANCING

Barbara loved colors and snow, squirrels and butterflies. She also loved music. She hummed her own tunes and learned to write them down in proper notes. Then she picked out the melody on the piano. For Christmas 1921, she was given two instruments, "one of percussion and the other of wood-wind": a triangle and a flageolet (a small flute, similar to a recorder).

She learned how to turn the flageolet into a piccolo. To play it, she wrote, "one has to force one's bottom lip against the bottom row of teeth, and one has to let one's upper lip hang over the hole in the side of the Piccolo, not quite touching it."

She eventually was given a violin, adding a stringed instrument to her musical collection. She wrote to Mr. Oberg that it was "exquisite, the G string was gut wound with wire, the D string was gut, the A string was gut also, and the E string was metal." Later she acquired cymbals. With these she pretended to be the percussion man while "mother plays the piano, and I have a time."

Barbara at eight with her violin, 1922.
[Barbara Newhall Follett papers, Columbia University Libraries]

Barbara danced and was very interested in costumes. She wrote to Mr. Oberg that she wore a Swedish outfit when she danced the Seven Jumps and the Crested Hen. The jacket she wore was "embroidered with worsted work, a little red frontpiece with a strip of black velvet across the top and a patch of beads on the front."

PRETEND FRIENDS AND
IMAGINARY WRITINGS

When Barbara was seven, she developed pretend friends. "I pretend that Beethoven, the Two Strausses, Wagner, and the rest of the composers . . . go skating with me, and when I invite them to dinner, a place has to be set for them; and when I have so many that the table won't hold them all, I make my family sit on one side of their chair to make room for them." All the composers had pretend maids, including Wagner's Katherine Loureena, who got her name because as a little girl "she loved to skate in the Arena."

When she was eight, Barbara built on her imagination and started to write a play called "The Fairy's Nest." It had thirteen fairies and a goblin who was "the worst enemy of the fairies." "I may have four acts," she explained, "or the third and fourth may be put together; I'm sure I don't know. It may even turn out to be a one act play."

She was also writing about eighteen imaginary birds. "The most interesting are the six finourios and the four fisheens. The finourios are all very pretty, but the knowraino finourio has the power to change his coat and also his song before it rains."

As always, she looked forward to summers at Sunapee. "I want as long as possible in that green, fairylike, woodsy, animal-filled, watery, luxuriant, butterfly-painted, moth-dotted, dragonfly-blotched, bird-filled, salamandous, mossy, ferny, sunshiny, moonshiny, long-dayful,

Barbara exploring outside at Lake Sunapee, 1922.

[Barbara Newhall Follett papers, Columbia University Libraries]

short-nightful land, oh that fishy, froggy, tadpoly, shelly, lizard-filled lake—oh, no end of lovely things to say about that place, and I am mad to get there."

Besides the birds, she wrote a series of stories about a princess; the first, "Verbiny and Her Kittens," was followed by "Verbiny and Her Butterflies" and "Verbiny and Her Birds." This led to her inventing a language. "In a chapter called Springtime," she wrote, "I have written down a little poem in a secret language that Verbiny called Farksoo."

Farksoo
Ar peen maiburs barge craik coo,
Peen yar fis farled cray pern.
Peen darndeon flar fooloos lart ain birdream.
Avee lart ain caireen
len tu cresteen der tuee,
Darnceen craik peen bune.

Barbara's translation
As the (maibur is a flower that comes in May and the plural is maiburs) begin to come,
The air is filled with perfume;
The dandelion fluff floats like a (birdream is something very lovely).
Also like a fairy in her dress of gold,
Dancing to the wind.

She wrote an interesting letter to children's book author Walter de la Mare that revealed something about her inspiration for writing. She loved his book *The Three Mulla-Mulgars* and wanted him to write a second adventure. "I have been waiting dreadfully long and *very* impatiently, and I should be so happy if you would hurry up and start it!"

Then she added, "I love the sound of your make-up words in the Mullas, and also the monkey talk. This must have been the cause of my making up a language called Farksoo."

FARKSOO AND FARKSOLIA

"The history of Farksolia," wrote Barbara, "is the account of my imaginary country—in fact, my imaginary *planet*. It is the history of the people who live here, the queens who ruled there, the flora that grow three—as well as a written map of continents, lakes, rivers, mountains, deserts, and cities. . . . As a matter of fact, there is a Farksoo language, too, which is carefully preserved on cards in drawers. . . . There are Farksolian letters, too, and sometimes I write mystic things, secret things, with them."

Farksoo was spoken in Farksolia. This land had eight seasons, two moons, and a beautiful sea with real mermaids. The trees had unusual warm sap and an ability to melt away snow and keep the mountains looking quite green.

"The Farksolian food consists largely of fruits and wild plants. Hardly any cooking is done. . . . One plant is very much like our celery in looks. A person going there would say: 'Pooh, this is only celery, I expected to have something marvelous.' Biting into it he would find the stalk filled with a red and purple juice in which flow little golden seeds."

The Farksolians lived together in one big city so they would not spoil the woodlands with houses everywhere. "In somewhere about the middle of the city there is an electric mail station. There runs from this mail station underground tunnels to every house. . . . The writing fluid is composed of the sap of a certain tree which is dark green in color. But of course it goes through several operations before it can be used."

Farksolia had, in succession, eleven queens, including Queen Bruwanderine, Queen Lacee, and Queen Flitterveen. Each was very beautiful in her own way. "Now for the queen's chamber!" wrote Barbara. "It had an arched ceiling of pure white material. The bed was made of silver and draped with gold. . . . The walls of the room were of silver ornamented with a great variety of precious stones. A little maiden dressed in blue and yellow was waiting for the queen to go to bed. She pulled open the bed, took out the roses which had lain there a while to keep the bed smelling sweetly; then the maiden pulled off the golden light and went out."

Not all was wonderful in Farksolia. Barbara wrote, "Queen Atee, the seventh, was chosen because of her beauty, but when she got to ruling she seemed too harsh for the people. So they waged the great Farksolian war against her and her friends. During this war the Farksolians were extinguished down to two families. One family has a little boy, and the other a little girl. The boy is about six years old, and the girl about six months. I hope that when they grow up they will marry and breed the race again."

Barbara asked Mr. Oberg to make illustrations of butterflies as she developed the land of Farksolia. She wished that she had a fairy camera to take pictures, but since she did not, she came up with very detailed descriptions. The daylight fuzzywing, for instance, was "so fuzzy that people call them fur-butterflies. . . . The female is plain white and curiously marked on the upper side with a nile green band around her neck, down on the part of the wing near the body, around in a curve, crossing itself, and touching her waist on each side, like this." Then she included a pencil sketch.

THE HOUSE WITHOUT WINDOWS

Three months before she turned nine, Barbara posted this typewritten notice on her door:

Nobody may come into this room
if the door is shut tight (if

```
it is shut not quite latched it
is all right) without knocking.
The person in this room if he
agrees that one shall come in
will say "come in," or some-
thing like that and if he does
not agree to it he will say "Not
yet, please," or something like
that. The door may be shut if
nobody is in the room but if a
person wants to come in, knocks
and hears no answer that means
that there is no one in the room
and he must not go in.
Reason. If the door is shut
tight and a person is in the
room the shut door means that
the person in the room wishes to
be left alone.
```

Then she got out a stack of paper and began to take the imaginary details from her mind and swirl them around into something new. By now she was an incredibly good typist capable of writing four thousand words in a day. Over the next three months she wrote an entire novel called *The House Without Windows and Eepersip's Life There.*

Mr. Oberg drew many butterflies to Barbara's exact specifications, including these
male and female blueetues. She loved them and wondered about his materials. "They
look to me like a mixture of crayons, oil painting, watercolors and some kind of varnish."
[Barbara Newhall Follett papers, Columbia University Libraries]

It was, she wrote to Mr. St. John, "about a little girl named
Eepersip who lived on top of a mountain, Mount Varcrobis, and was
so lonely that she went to live wild. She talked to the animals, and led
a sweet lovely life with them—just the kind of life that I should like
to lead. Her parents all tried to catch her, with some friends of theirs,
and every time she escaped in some way or other. . . . She played

games with butterflies! . . . She often thought that she was going to learn from end to beginning butterfly history."

That summer of 1923 at Sunapee, Barbara revised the book amid swimming, canoeing, and mountain climbing. Her father thought that nine-year-old Barbara's homeschool education could be expanded

As Sabra turned one, Barbara wrote to Mr. Oberg, "If you could see Sabra, you'd certainly see something that would make you feel happy."
[Barbara Newhall Follett papers, Columbia University Libraries]

to learn about printing, proofs, and proofreading, the work of creating an actual book. Maybe she could construct a few books and hand them out to her friends?

It was also the summer when Barbara met her baby sister, Sabra. Barbara described the baby at six months old as a sweet sister, "growing more lively every day. She loves to look at her own tiny pink hands . . . loves to sit up straight. . . . Probably she will discover something new everyday."

Barbara later wrote to Mr. St. John, "Eepersip got so wild that she could receive messages from the fairies, and one day they came to her clutching her dress and kneeling before her and telling her that she had a sister, five years old, and her name was Eeverine. And Eepersip went back to her old house and without mercy on the parents she took Eeverine away, to live wild with her!"

FIRE!

In 1923, the day after the family returned from Sunapee to their home, a kerosene burner on the kitchen stove exploded. The fire destroyed all of Barbara's manuscripts, including the recently revised forty-thousand-word manuscript of *The House Without Windows*. It also consumed her violin, stuffed animals, clothes, and all other possessions. Fortunately the baby just missed being badly burned. With no insurance, the family was left without a place to live and in a financial bind.

Barbara's mother, Helen, wrote to Mr. St. John about the fire: "Barbara has been a brick about it all; she has suffered as only a sensitive person can suffer, but she has been absolutely silent about it. She became immediately absorbed in Shelley, and has gone quite wild over his poems. The only thing she wants for Christmas is a trip to the sea, a whole day at the sea where it is particularly lonesome and wild." Barbara attended a lecture at Yale on Percy Shelley, an important English poet. She then wrote to the professor that she had "never been able, never known how to express what I think and feel about Shelley; and now you have quite wonderfully done it for me!"

But her destroyed novel was always in her mind. She wrote that "for many days I tried to rewrite and could not, but after a while I got a sudden inspiration, and I am now working on it like fire." She also expanded her dictionary for the Farksoo language, making separate cards for each word.

Grandmother Ding got a letter saying that the rewrite was making the book better "with lots of things taken out and more put in. I think you may remember that in my first Eepersip some of the plans the family made to catch Eepersip were too fancy and ingenious, these plans are much more simple and I think more to the interest of the reader."

Over the next couple of years, Barbara went on an extended canoe trip with her father and worked on the revisions when she could. She began writing to a neighbor across the lake, George Bryan, who had fun with her interest in Peter Pan and pirates. He wrote:

In 1924, Barbara wrote to Mr. St. John, "The best event of this
hectic summer was—a week's camping trip alone with Daddy."
[Barbara Newhall Follett papers, Columbia University Libraries]

To One Styling Himself PETER PAN:

You must have One Thousand Dollars ($1,000) *in gold* deposited at the foot of the pine tree at the spot known as your Pine House, not later than 11:30 o'clock p.m., E.S.T., on Saturday, July 25th, 1925.

This is final!

James Hook

Captain of the Avenging Angels

Barbara, always busy with piano and violin lessons, schoolwork, and keeping a log on Sabra, finally got the manuscript for *The House Without Windows* rewritten when she was twelve. Her father now decided that it was something that might be published. He helped her submit it to Knopf in New York City, where he worked. Barbara waited anxiously for news. These words finally came from Blanche Knopf, vice president of the publishing house:

"This is to let you know that I have just finished reading your manuscript and like it enormously. Of course we want to publish it and hope to if you will let us."

Barbara responded: "Again let me tell you how thankful I am—how delighted—how astonished, that you are going to *publish* it—my little story."

There was still work to be done, and Barbara corrected her own galley proofs for errors. Finally the book was printed and ready for release on January 21, 1927. Before the book was actually in the stores, all twenty-five hundred copies were sold out. Barbara's father wrote, "I hope you will get a moment's pleasure out of learning that the second printing of *The House Without Windows* is ordered to-day, just ten days before publication. We shall try to make you a new and better jacket to-morrow."

Reviews came pouring in.

"This is very beautiful writing. But there are moments when for one reader, this book grows almost unbearably beautiful. It becomes

Publicity photo for *The House Without Windows*. [Stefan Cooke, Farksolia.org]

an ache in the throat," wrote Lee Wilson Dodd in the *Saturday Review of Literature*.

"*The House Without Windows* will interest anybody who cares a snap of his fingers for beauty and good writing. . . . The author has never been to school. There seems to be no sane reason why she should ever go to one unless she wants to. . . . She writes as though she were living in that serene abode where the eternal are. . . . That is where she lives and where she takes us," wrote Howard Mumford Jones in the *New York World*.

Jones also wrote that the book was inspiring his daughter to run away. Barbara responded: "But tell Eleanor to cheer up and finish the book. I have many plans up my sleeve for an Eepersipian escape, and I should be very glad to have a comrade—especially Eleanor."

One reviewer, however, Anne Carroll Moore, head of the children's library services for the New York Public Library system, wrote that she could "conceive of no greater handicap for the writer between the ages of nineteen and thirty-nine, than to have published a successful book between the ages of nine and twelve. . . . What price will Barbara Follett have to pay for her 'big days' at the typewriter, days when she rattles off, we are told, four to five thousand words of original copy at a speed of 1,200 words to the hour, producing at the end of three months a complete story of some 40,000 words. I have only words of praise for the story itself."

Barbara wrote a scathing response. "I wrote the story in the first place because I wanted to run away, but, realizing the impossibility of it, I made someone else do it for me. The book was not written to be published—it was written for the sheer joy of writing. . . . You also said: 'Children need the companionship of other children'—but you seem to take it perfectly for granted that I do not. What made you think that? For I do play with other children and up to a certain point I like it. It is undeniable that I do not go to parties and social events as much as other children do, but that, from my point of view, is *not* a forfeit. . . . It is by my own free will."

In addition to her writing, Barbara maintained a serious interest in music and dancing. She was taking a violin lesson from the dean of music at Yale when she discovered that her technique was flawed. "I was standing wrong; my bow-arm was wrong; my fingers of the left hand were good, but the left arm (wrist and elbow) were not. And so a single forty-five minutes undid all but a small fraction of what I had woven with such care."

Piano and violin lessons were part of her homeschooling. Here is a sample homeschool assignment from March 6, 1924.

I. Practice on the piano. You must have a good lesson for Bruce. See if an hour of practice is too much. Remember that the other children in school don't have this chance of getting in some good music during the early part of the day.

II. At ten o'clock begin the following French: Review lesson 28, see if you can write the forms of the verb given in that lesson. . . .

Review the poem you memorized, and try writing it. Then learn the vocabulary under lesson 29. This will get you ready for me to take up lesson 29 with you. Time yourself in doing this French. Use every moment hard.

III. At about 11 o'clock begin your violin. Time this also, and tell me exactly how long you can keep at it well. I imagine that an hour on the piano would not be too much, but that an hour on the violin would be.

IV. Page 89 of your Arithmetic book do over again examples 17, 20, 21, 23, 24, 26, 27. I am anxious to get through with this commission business and get into interest with you—banking, etc. But we can't get along until you have got the idea of discounts and commissions.

V. This is a good morning's work. See that the work you do is neat enough to show to Mr. Oberg. Let him see what kind of lessons we can do when we get started. This afternoon is your play-class, remember.

THE PIRATE CRAZE AND A LOST FATHER

Barbara wrote to Mr. St. John that he might think she was faithless to Eepersip and nature but "all the same, I am wild over PIRATES— their unknown islands, masses of blood-drenched gold, mystic maps, wild seas, wild fights, wild deeds!" She wrote a narrative poem that "contains everything from Blackbeard to myself, from poppies to sea-shells, from butterflies to pieces of eight, from ghosts to living pirates, from maps to palm-trees."

In her "sea-rage" phase, Barbara heard about a schooner called the *Frederick H.* in the harbor. "Going down to see her almost every day, that I could think of nothing else, let alone write letters." The ship delivered a load of lumber and was scheduled to return to Nova Scotia in a few days. Quickly Barbara managed to join the crew, with Mr. Bryan (her James Hook correspondent) along as a chaperone.

She wrote again to Mr. St. John: "Oh! there is nothing in the world more thoroughly delightful than being under sails, the schooner leaning before a north-west gale, the green and foaming waves raging all about, the sails full and bellowing out with wind, the howling and whistling of wind through the white canvas."

When the weather changed, everything was "rolling and thumping, doors banging in the cabin, bottles and dishes jingling, the groaning of the booms as they would swing in and out, the billowing and flapping of the idle sails, the pattering of reef-points . . . with watches, lookouts, two-hour tricks, the merry yarning of the crew when off duty in the fo'c'sle, the gayness of them all, the carefreeness—it was all just exactly as I had dreamed."

Barbara insisted on learning everything possible about the ship, working with the crew and cook, and studying the engine. "And I loved to go up in the rigging, too," she wrote, "especially on hot days. . . . Up and up I would go, into the taut ratlines, feeling the life and joy of the ship as if she were a living, happy creature . . . up where the taut ratlines quivered a little beneath the strain of the wind, and I would sit on the cross-trees and swing my legs into space."

After this experience in June 1927, Barbara wrote a fourteen-page account of the adventure, which became her second book, *The Voyage of the Norman D.* It was published in 1928, when she was fourteen.

"Barbara's *The Voyage of the Norman D.* is as amazing a creation in realism for a twelve years' child as *The House Without Windows* was amazing in fantasy for a nine years'. I see the same gifts, however, in each: the child's zest for living, changing normally from fantasy to realism. . . . It is complete, zestful transmutation of her child's experience into amazing effective language. . . . For the first time in history, it would seem the abounding healthy child has become the authentic child-artist," wrote William Leonard, an English professor at the University of Wisconsin.

"Through the whole telling of the voyage, as exciting in the telling as any buccaneer yarn, one finds the same fervor of description, the same untiring joy in living and keen reaction to natural beauty as in the earlier book," said Margery Williams Bianco, author of *The Velveteen Rabbit*, in the *Saturday Review of Literature*.

Barbara made many friends among the seamen and captains and

As sailing ships were replaced by steamers, Barbara fell in love with the last
of the masted schooners and explored them from top to bottom.
Here she is high up in the rigging of the *Carnegie*, a research vessel with
eight sailors and seven scientists.

[Barbara Newhall Follett papers, Columbia University Libraries]

started writing to them. It was a very different experience from her usual connections with academic people. Here is one letter:

Will Shipmate
reiced you letter was glad to here form you again will I have home all summer the Frederick H. must be in Boston now the cook is hur the capen is home you sed you wish I could see your Ship I spose you are capen now . . . how is your Father and Mother give them my best wishes will ship mate I will close hoping to here form you soon
your shipmate
Bill

That same year her father, off working for Knopf in New York, fell in love with his secretary and left the family. Barbara was devastated. She wrote to him: "I depend very much on you: and I trust you to give another heave to the capstan bars, to get the family anchor started toward the surface again. . . . You don't want the family anchor to remain forever on the bottom, do you?"

Her father never came back, and the parting was not friendly. Helen refused to divorce him, and with his state of mind, his living situation, and the depressed job market, he had a rough time getting steady work. Eventually he read scripts for the movie studio MGM.

He preferred not to be found. When he was being considered for a literary prize, he refused to let a coworker tell the awards committee where he was.

He wrote that the prize wasn't worth it to him. "You see, I've run away from my wife, who is a dreadful termagant. You may be able to understand how I feel about her when I say that in order to be free, I have had to abandon my daughter."

Helen wrote that Barbara's words against her father were "very very bitter." Barbara took a train by herself to visit him, but he was not friendly. She then caught another train and went to stay with friends for a week without telling her mother.

Interestingly, before his marriage to Helen, her father sent one child, Grace, to live with his parents after his first wife died. And after leaving Helen, Barbara, and Sabra, he eventually married his secretary, had three more children, and left that family, too.

OFF TO THE WEST INDIES AND BEYOND

Barbara became very interested in a famous research schooner called the *Carnegie*. It was specially outfitted for scientific studies and had been making oceanic research trips for many years. Barbara convinced her mother that they should follow this ship on its next journey to various islands in the Caribbean Sea. The study was focused on copepods, minute crustaceans related to crabs.

With her husband gone and Helen needing to make a living, she

Barbara became fascinated with the *Carnegie* and its research. She is in the far right
foreground seeing the ship off at Newport News, Virginia. [Stefan Cooke, Farksolia.org]

thought they might be able to earn some money writing travel articles.
Helen wrote, "Barbara's job with Harper is still on, and we start with her
five hundred dollar royalties plus some more money of hers accruing from
her books, making in all something over a thousand dollars." When
they packed up to go, two typewriters were included in the luggage.

Helen, however, left without any commitment from a publisher for an advance contract and received only $50 to write about the educational aspects of the trip. She was hoping to get money from Wilson, but he was against the trip, had no job, and never sent any. He did, however, offer to edit and market any writings that they might send him. Barbara and her mother traveled from 1928 to 1929. During this time Sabra was left in the care of friends.

Barbara did not complete a book in the year of travel. Possibly it was to be about Farksolia or pirates, but nothing survives. She did have a commission from William Hornaday, the man credited with saving the American bison, to find out what was happening to the golden plover in the tropics. She was also asked to find out about bugs. And Barbara was intrigued to learn more about steamers and sailing ships as they sailed around. She wrote about costumes, dances, rituals, religion, trees, birds, and butterflies on Saint Lucia, Saint Kitts, Trinidad, and other islands.

Here are a few lines from a poem written about Barbados.

Darkness and mystery.
The moon shining
Upon the white, deserted streets.
A heavy, rich fragrance
From thousands of tropic blossoms.
Leaf-patterns from the guava-tree
Upon the white coral pavement.
A palm against the sky—stately—solemn.
Silence.

Only the countless, innumerable voices

Of cricket, beetle, cicada,

All blended in one shrill, chirping note.

They sing without pause or fall.

The island's heart is singing.

Eventually the $500 advance to Barbara for a book she had not yet written was used to finance part of the trip. There was a lot of stress about finances and writing, and Barbara had a breakdown in

Barbara and her mother on their travels. [Stefan Cooke, Farksolia.org]

the South Seas. Not many details are known about this, but she and her mother headed back to the United States.

While returning by ship from Honolulu to California, Barbara met a shipmate, referred to as A. They became very attached. Barbara wrote that she was discouraged because some of her dearest friends seemed to be in deep trouble, and she couldn't do anything about it. "Perhaps that is why," she said, referring to her father as WF, "I cling for dear life to A. He, with no tools and no material, has nevertheless made something most beautiful and real out of life. . . . I'll never forget or forgive WF's attitude toward him. That was mainly what caused the sharp and sudden break between him and me. It was unwarranted, ridiculous and mean. My respect for WF did its loudest blowing-up over that. . . . A. is a treasure." A. often sailed off to Point Barrow in the Arctic, but they kept in contact for three years with letters, sometimes three a week.

Once Barbara and her mother reached California, Barbara stayed with two women friends near Pasadena, where she enrolled in a community college and spent time with her father. It was agreed that Barbara and her mother should be apart for a while, and Helen went back to Hawaii to work on her book called *Magic Portholes*. Many bills were owed, and there was talk of divorce. Barbara escaped from the situation to Northern California and for a while was detained as a runaway. This was in all the newspapers and forced Helen to return from Honolulu to deal with it.

Barbara made new friends on her own. One of them, the writer

Alice Russell, clipped off Barbara's long braids on her sixteenth birthday and gave her a fashionable bob. Barbara called the haircut "one of the best afternoon's works I ever accomplished—or perhaps ever shall." These California friends became "the inspiration to my failing courage, and their spiritual splicing of my main brace." During this time she said she didn't have "the gumption of a weevil in a biscuit. . . . Really, I'm not worth the respect of a mosquito." Then she added: "But I'm happy as I can be!"

When Barbara and Helen eventually made it back to the East Coast, they spent two months working on *Magic Portholes*. Macmillan published it in 1932, illustrated by Armstrong Sperry. Barbara, who came up with the title and helped in many other ways, was never given any credit for her part in this book or other collaborations that she did with her mother.

While the two shared living space, Barbara wrote that Helen was not doing well. "She's underwater. God! And I can't rescue her. I do forty-nine fiftieths of everything that is done at No. 122." When she finally saw Sabra after a two-year absence, Barbara wrote, "I rushed to her with my heart wide open, and my soul ready for the balm I felt she'd give—and the beautiful dream melted, and I found a little child—a darling little child, to be sure—who took all I could give, and gave almost nothing in return, because she *could* not, of course."

Barbara wrote that she was going to New York with "six chances to get a job there. . . . My idea of Heaven right now is a place where one can get work without hiking the streets to look for it! . . . One has to

Alice Russell and Barbara on her sixteenth birthday with a new haircut.

[Barbara Newhall Follett papers, Columbia University Libraries]

whang, and bang, and hunt, and explore, and suffer, and grow shields and javelins and such-like in the process. . . . When the steam pressure got up, there was no doubt what to do about it—'write to A.' . . . There never was a safer, solider, more rock-like person in the world!"

A WRITER GOES SILENT

Barbara did not finish her own book, and at age sixteen, during the Great Depression, entered the job market in New York City owing money to her publisher. She went to stenographer school, which taught a quick method to take notes, and enjoyed it after the first few days. She also did typing for hire. Eventually she managed to get a very good job. "Taking letters in shorthand is still quite a glamorous proceding to me. . . . I like the people that I work with—we all get along admirably well. . . . After November 7th, I think it will be full-time, at twenty-five a week, or thereabouts. This is a remarkably good wage for a person so inexperienced as I."

She wrote about A., who was off for four months in the Arctic: "A. and I commune continually; we nibble delicately at the earth as though it were a piece of cheese. . . . We get along, though it's very unsatisfactory not to be together."

Then in the summer of 1931, while vacationing with her mother in Vermont, she worked on her story "Lost Island." She also met several new friends from the local college and began to get back into mountain hikes, especially with a young man whom she called S. His name was Nickerson Rogers.

In 1932, at age eighteen, Barbara quit her job in New York, stopped communicating with her mother, and broke off with A., who was spending another summer in the Arctic. Barbara put "Lost Island" out on the market and then made a return to nature with Nick Rogers. He had been visiting her over the winter and spring of 1931–32. They camped in New England and then sailed off to Spain, from there traveling to the Alps and the Black Forest in Germany. This was the beginning of a seven-year relationship. When they married, Barbara changed her name to Barbara Rogers. She also spent time again with her mother and father during this period.

Very little is known about these years because Barbara rarely wrote letters and did not seem to be doing any writing. Eventually she and Nick settled down to work in Boston. Barbara went back to typing and stenographer jobs. She also wrote synopses for Fox Films. Nick, on the other hand, began to experience some financial success as an engineer. On July 9, 1939, Barbara wrote, "S. is about the only one I know who has a job, likes it, expects to keep it, and is earning a modest living wage! If I can just hang on to him I ought to be O.K. Whether or not I can remains to be seen! This winter I had a bad spell, made a mess of things, and have some ground to recover!"

Nick was often away from home on business trips and had less time to get out in the mountains. Barbara decided to dance with a semi-professional group. In the summer of 1939 she drove with friends to

Barbara at camp in 1932. [Stefan Cooke, Farksolia.org]

California for several weeks of advanced instruction at Mills College. She was also able to see her friend Alice. On the second day of the visit a shattering letter arrived from Nick. He wasn't sure if he wanted to stay together.

Barbara hurried back to Boston, but Nick wasn't there. After several days he returned to their apartment. "The thing is really worse than I had thought possible," she wrote. "There IS somebody else." Nick agreed to try to work things out, and they went to Cape Cod for the weekend.

Barbara and Nick moved to a better apartment. "On the surface things are terribly, terribly calm, and wrong—just as wrong as they can be," Barbara wrote. "I still think there is a chance that the outcome will be a happy one; but I would have to think that anyway, in order to live; so you can draw any conclusion you like from that!"

On Thursday, December 7, 1939, in the early evening, Barbara walked out of her Brookline apartment. She was twenty-five years old. She had about $30 with her and the shorthand notes she had taken during the day. She was never seen again.

Nick did not report her missing for two weeks. When he did make a report, the Bureau of Missing Persons sent out a five-state alarm but found nothing. In 1941, her father published an eight-page anonymous article in the May issue of the *Atlantic Monthly* titled "To a Daughter, One Year Lost." "A year!" he wrote. "It is very strange to reflect that two Christmases have come and gone . . . since any one of us who love you has clasped your hand or received a syllable written by it or unearthed the smallest clue to where you are, even to whether you are living or dead."

He reminisced about ten days they'd spent above the tree line in a misty winter with frost ferns and frozen cranberries. He scolded, praised, and gave advice. "But let me remind you of this," he wrote. "You were a great person. . . . You were born one. It is pretty safe to say that no one ever questioned that who has known you, or read those still radiant early books of yours, or received your letters. . . . You were to all others a very synonym of generous freedom, the ardent spirit, the courage to be oneself. . . . Can you not, without sacrifice to anything vital to you, at least choose one of us and cause him to receive for us all the basic reassurance that you live, that you are where you want to be and doing what you want to do, that there is nothing (if so it must be) that anyone can do for you?"

Not one word was ever heard from Barbara. Because Missing Persons listed her as Barbara Rogers, the literary community did not realize for twenty-five years that she was gone. Everyone who knew her kept her letters. Eventually this material was gathered into a collection at Columbia University. Barbara's half-nephew, Stefan Cooke, put together a six-hundred-page book called *Barbara Newhall Follett: A Life in Letters*. It includes letters, short stories, poems, photographs, and much more. He also maintains a website, Farksolia.org, where *The House Without Windows*, the unpublished "Lost Island," and much other material may be read or downloaded.

Stefan says, "I have many questions about my family history, but the question that stands out among them, by far, is, What happened to Barbara Follett next?"

CHAPTER 4

Amelia Earhart, the Lost Legend

Please know I am quite aware of the hazards.
I want to do it because I want to do it.
Women must try to do things as men have tried.
When they fail, their failure must be
but a challenge to others.
—Amelia Earhart

RISING TO THE TOP

THE 1930S WAS THE ERA of the Great Depression, with World War II threatening to erupt. It was a time before television and the internet propelled people to instant celebrity. Still, a woman in an unusual and dangerous occupation managed to bedazzle the public as she worked her way up, up, up, to worldwide fame.

It wasn't because she was highly skilled as a photographer, clothing designer, and compassionate social worker. It wasn't even because she was a terrific writer of bestselling books, an inspiring lecturer, and a great friend of First Lady Eleanor Roosevelt.

She became famous as a daring pilot, setting one record after another in the early days of air travel. Like other pioneers in aviation history, she experienced failing engines, crumpled wings, and too many crashes. But this was her passion. She tried again and again to be the first and fastest across oceans and continents until she flew toward a tiny speck of an island in the vast Pacific Ocean. Somewhere on this 2,556-mile flight, she and her navigator went missing without a trace.

That was more than eighty years ago. Today her fate continues to be one of the most intriguing mysteries in the world. Books and documentaries are still being written, new theories explored, more expeditions outfitted for yet another search.

How did it all start? Will we ever know for sure how it ended?

Amelia flying in a storm.

"FIRST TIME THINGS"

Amelia Earhart was born on July 24, 1897, in Kansas. She was three when her younger sister, Muriel, arrived. At that time her parents sent Amelia off to live about fifty miles away with her wealthy and proper maternal grandparents. They had a nine-room house with maids and a cook, horses and a garden, a piano, and plenty of books.

Amelia was a dreamer, always looking for adventure in her life. Her mother described her as "highly imaginative" with a "strong,

Amelia at age three holding her eight-month-old sister, Muriel, taken around the time Amelia was sent to live with her grandmother. [Schlesinger Library, Radcliffe Institute]

self-sufficient streak." As a child, she was often doing things others thought she shouldn't, or couldn't, do. Grandmother Otis wanted ladylike behavior, such as no fence climbing and no mud on clothes. Amelia, however, liked "first time things." She invented recipes and games for her guests to try something new.

Amelia, known as Millie, had three best friends—Ginger, Toot, and Katch. They were often together and loved to roller-skate, play baseball, and explore musty caves along the Missouri River.

Toot said that Millie "was always the instigator. She would dare anything, and we would all follow along." Amelia described their favorite game of Bogie. "It was played in my grandmother's barn and consisted of taking imaginary journeys to deepest Africa and darkest Asia in an old abandoned carriage." Amelia studied maps and atlases as they "trekked" through jungles and deserts.

Amelia's mother, Amy Otis Earhart, had bloomers made for her daughters so that they wouldn't have to play in the skirts typical of the time. Amelia collected moths, katydids, and toads, and even kept a cow skull in her bedroom. When she did play with dolls, she designed and sewed clothes for them. Both sisters liked to read and had a clever way to fit it into their busy days. While one did chores, the other read aloud from a book.

Amelia attended a tiny school with only forty students. She was a good student who loved to read western thrillers or novels of Charles Dickens. But she did not care for the children's books in her grandmother's library. "They were all about very good little boys and

Amelia (on stilts) and Muriel (on the swing) wearing bloomers.

[Schlesinger Library, Radcliffe Institute]

girls emerging triumphant over very bad little boys and girls," she said. They reminded her of "dull sermons."

In the summers, Amelia spent more time with her parents and sister. In 1904, when she was seven, the family went to the Saint Louis World's Fair. A Ferris wheel was featured along with horse races, animals, and vegetable displays. She begged for a ride on the roller coaster, but her mother cautioned, "It's too dangerous for little girls." Amelia decided that she, Muriel, and friends needed a roller coaster. Using fence boards, lard, baby-buggy wheels, and a wooden crate, she built a slick ride from the top of a wood shed to the grass below. When Amelia tried it out, she slammed into the ground and ended up with a bruised lip and torn clothes. This did not stop her. She redesigned the angle of the slope and loved the improved ride. It felt "just like flying," she said. However, Grandmother Otis said it was dangerous, and soon it was torn down.

LESS HAPPY TIMES

When she was eleven, Amelia joined her parents and sister in Des Moines, Iowa. Her father, Edwin, had found a job working for the Rock Island Railroad. They moved four times in four years, each time to a better house. But he began to drink heavily, and sometimes her parents were separated.

When Amelia was in high school, her grandmother died. Because of her father's drinking, a huge estate that should have gone partially to her mother went into a trust. Her father drank even more and was eventually fired. Amelia came up with money-saving ideas such as walking instead of taking the bus. She also made Easter outfits for herself and Muriel from old curtains.

In the turmoil Amelia went to six different high schools. At sixteen she looked worried and thin, and her grades dropped. She had no friends. In 1914, Amelia's mother decided to leave her father and took her daughters to live with friends in Chicago. Amelia attended Hyde Park High School, where she was described in the yearbook as "the girl in brown who walks alone."

Her mother went to court to regain her inheritance, and using some of this money, nineteen-year-old Amelia enrolled at the Ogontz School for Young Ladies near Philadelphia. It provided one of the best college-preparatory programs around for women. Amelia played hockey and wrote her mother that she had made two goals. She studied German, French, drama, and logic. Like most young ladies of the time, she also learned proper ways to walk, bow, sit, and stand. As secretary of the Red Cross chapter, she started a surgical dressing course, and when it came time to buy class rings, she thought the money should go instead to the Red Cross.

In 1917, Amelia visited Muriel, who was going to school in Toronto, Canada. It was during World War I, and the streets were full of wounded soldiers. Instead of going back to school, Amelia decided to be useful and volunteer as a nurse's aide at Spadina Military Hospital.

Amelia as a nurse's aide in Toronto.

[Schlesinger Library, Radcliffe Institute]

The work was strenuous. She took care of patients from 7:00 a.m. to 7:00 p.m., with two hours off in the afternoon. She became friends with a British pilot and also a woman who designed clothes. Some of her free time was spent watching pilots perform training maneuvers. The stunts were exciting and amazing, and she felt her "first urge to fly."

Before long she was also helping people during the terrible flu pandemic of 1918. World War I claimed twenty million lives, but this illness sickened five hundred million around the world, and up to fifty million people died as a result.

Amelia was wearing down. She got terribly ill herself with a sinus infection that required surgery and hospitalization. In a time before antibiotics, her illness became a serious chronic condition that returned many times in her life.

When the war ended, Amelia enrolled as a premed student at Columbia University in New York City. She fed orange juice to mice and learned how to dissect a cockroach, which she said had "an extraordinarily large brain!" Deciding she would rather do research than work with patients, she left the program. She seemed at a crossroads in knowing what to do. She tried several things, including a course in automotive repair.

In 1920, her parents got back together for a while, and she joined them in California. She went to an air show with her father, who paid $1 for her to fly over the Hollywood Hills. After just a few enthralling moments in the air, with wind in her face and a panorama below, she was hooked.

Amelia Earhart knew she had to fly!

THE BRIGHT YELLOW *CANARY*

In 1920, the United States Post Office hired forty pilots for airmail delivery. By the end of the year, fifteen of those pilots had died in crashes because the motors "would drop out without warning." Amelia, however, admitted that "the danger made it all the more thrilling." She was determined to start flying lessons.

Amelia got a job in the mailroom of a telephone company. Her father objected, but Amelia quietly saved money to take flight lessons from a twenty-four-year-old female instructor named Neta Snook. In 1920, it was unusual for anyone to be in aviation, let alone a woman, but Snook had managed to become a licensed pilot and was running her own flight business. She even knew how to rebuild a biplane.

On weekends Amelia took an hour's ride on a streetcar and then walked several miles to reach the airfield. To fit in better with the male-dominated world of aviation, she wore breeches and a leather coat. She also started cutting her own hair, a little bit here, a little bit there, until she had a short style that she curled into a bob.

Flying was complicated, but Amelia found ways to "play around in the air." With a wide-open cockpit, she wore a leather cap over her ears and goggles to protect her eyes. Soon she could make turns, keep the wings level, reduce wobbling, and then make a smooth landing. Neta noted that she did make mistakes, including not checking the fuel level and daydreaming in the air.

After two and a half hours of lessons Amelia decided that she needed her own plane. Neta, after all, was a good instructor, but she

Amelia with flying goggles and a leather cap.
[Putnam Collection of Amelia Earhart Papers]

was providing lessons in a clunky old warplane, a Curtiss Canuck. Amelia wanted something much more sporty, a plane that could take off quickly, climb steeply, and go faster.

With all her savings and some help from her mother and sister, she bought a bright yellow Kinner Airster biplane. It was called the *Canary*. It cost twice as much as a used Canuck, so she needed to work more. As much as possible she loaned the plane out to avoid charges for storage in a hangar. One of her multiple jobs included driving a gravel truck. After working in a photo studio, she started carrying a small camera everywhere.

She switched to a new instructor and added barnstorming tricks until she could dive, execute loop-de-loops and barrel rolls, and pull out of a spiral straight down toward the ground.

The *Canary* had no instrument panels. This meant the only way Amelia would know if she was flying upside down in fog was when her feet dropped off the rudders and the seat belt tightened. In this risky business, Amelia had her share of crashes. Once her motor cut out, and she landed in a cabbage patch. Then she ended up in a muddy field and bit her tongue. At another time her wheels stuck, and the plane tipped over.

Despite these "little crack ups," Amelia still loved flying. She was focused on safety and learned whatever she could from engineers. She also pushed the limits. In 1922, Amelia became the first woman to fly at an altitude of fourteen thousand feet and set off on an aviation career that eventually broke many records.

SOCIAL WORK

In 1924, when her parents finally divorced, Amelia decided to move to Boston with her mother and sister. In California she sold the *Canary* and bought a bright yellow touring car, which earned the name Yellow Peril because of Amelia's driving habits. She and her mother set off on a rambling, seven-thousand-mile journey across the continent. Once in Boston, Amelia found work at Denison House, in a job that she really liked.

Amelia's car, the Yellow Peril. [Schlesinger Library, Radcliffe Institute]

There, Amelia helped immigrant children, mainly Chinese and Syrian, learn English and settle into new lives. For appointments, or just for the fun of it, she gave them rides in the Yellow Peril. She had more sinus surgeries but still had abundant energy and many new ideas for this career as a social worker. She worked with education and social groups such as the Syrian Mothers' Club. She taught children how to play basketball and how to fence. To raise awareness, she flew a plane over the city and dropped pamphlets about Denison House.

Chosen as a delegate to a conference in Boston, she was recognized as one of the most influential social workers of her generation. She might have worked there for years, except something unexpected happened.

"A SACK OF POTATOES"

In 1928, Amelia received a phone call. A World War I army captain, Hilton H. Railey, asked if she would like to do "something for aviation which might be hazardous." He would not tell her what it was until she met him in person later that day: "Would you fly the Atlantic?"

The plan involved a Fokker plane called the *Friendship*. The plane had pontoons instead of wheels so it could land on water. It was painted bright orange so it could be easily spotted. Explorer Richard E. Byrd had originally ordered the plane to use for his planned flight over the

South Pole but ultimately chose a Ford plane when Edsel Ford became a sponsor of the expedition.

A wealthy woman, Amy Phipps Guest, had recently leased the *Friendship* and was hoping to become the first woman to fly across the Atlantic Ocean. She tried to keep her plans secret, but her family found out. Since nineteen people, including two women passengers, had died trying to accomplish this feat, they begged her to stop. She relented but told her lawyer to find an American lady, "college-educated, attractive and, if possible, a flyer" to do it. She would pay the bills.

A well-known publisher named George Putnam heard about this offer. "I had stumbled on an adventure-in-the-making which might provide a book." He looked for more information. Eventually Amelia was interviewed and offered the position. Amelia, always interested in "first time things," agreed.

Amelia had five hundred hours of flight time, and she was also tall and lanky, and resembled the great aviation hero Charles Lindbergh. The year before, Lindbergh had become the first pilot to successfully fly solo across the Atlantic Ocean, from New York to Paris. He landed amid what a reporter described as "thousand of hands weaving like maggots over the silver wings of the *Spirit of Saint-Louis*." George Putnam published and helped Lindbergh promote a bestselling book about his transatlantic flight.

Amelia was made captain of the flight that would cross the Atlantic Ocean from Trepassey, Newfoundland, to Southampton,

England. She joined pilot Bill Stultz, mechanic Louis "Slim" Gordon, and backup pilot Louis Gower in Boston Harbor, where the *Friendship* was moored. Amelia intended to do some of the flying, but the weather would require steering by instruments, a skill she did not yet have.

Twice a tugboat took them out to the plane moored in the harbor, but it was bad weather and a "no go." Part of the problem was weight. "Out went six five-gallon cans of gasoline," wrote Amelia. Gower also stayed behind. When the *Friendship* was finally able to rev up its engines, screech across the water, and get airborne, the cabin door slid open. Amelia dived for a gas can and almost fell out.

They made it to Trepassey and waited another thirteen days for the right conditions. The heavy surf and spray kept drowning the outboard motors. To get into the air again they had to leave much more behind: life jackets, a rubber dingy, and all luggage. They even dumped all but seven hundred gallons of fuel, which was just enough to get to Ireland.

When they were finally in the air, Amelia spent much of her time looking out the window at fog, clouds, and the "gulping beauty" of a pink sunset. She ate oranges and some malted milk balls while they went through a snowstorm and more fog. The huge egg sandwiches and coffee she left "to the boys." She wore a man's fur-lined suit. It was a size 40, full of pockets and much too big for her, but it provided warmth in a plane with no heat. During the night she tried to write in the blackness. The plane was so shaky that she had to use her left thumb to keep the pencil in a straight line.

When dawn broke, the left engine was coughing, the radio was dead, and they had only a one-hour supply of gas. Something was seriously wrong. They should have reached land long ago.

The pilot saw the transport steamer *America* and headed toward it. But with the dead radio, they couldn't make contact. Amelia scribbled a note asking the steamer crew to paint its latitude and longitude position on the deck. Then she dropped the note from the plane in a bag weighed down with an orange. However, the wind swooped it up and the bag plopped into the water. With the last orange she tried again . . . but no luck.

Now the pilot had to make a decision. Should they land in the ocean and have the steamer pick them up? Or should they keep on? They decided to stick to the course. Before Amelia closed the hatch, she took a photograph of the *America*. It was the first photo of a vessel at sea made from a transatlantic flight.

Finally after twenty hours and forty minutes in the air, they saw a blue shadow. Land! The *Friendship* managed to land on the water and tie up to a buoy off Burry Port, Wales. No one was expecting them, and Amelia waved a towel to attract some attention. *Hello? Hello?*

Finally someone noticed, and as the story came out, Amelia's life took an incredible turn. Here she was, the first woman to fly across the Atlantic Ocean. As Amelia, Bill, and Slim made their way to

Amelia at the door of the *Friendship*'s cabin after it finally
arrived in Southampton, England.

Southampton and on to London, tugboats whistled, foghorns blared, and people cheered on the streets. Amelia, who preferred to be alone, found herself directly in the public eye.

Even though she insisted that Bill and Slim had done all the work—that she was "a sack of potatoes"—she became a star, a very big star. When people found out that her luggage consisted of two scarves, a comb, and a toothbrush, she was given free shopping sprees. She sailed back to New York with three trunks of new clothes and gifts. In London, she also bought a new plane, an Avro Avian, from Lady Mary Heath, who had just flown it in a daring solo trip from South Africa. During the sail, she became friends with the ship's captain, Harry Manning, who talked navigation with her. He would later become involved when she decided to fly around the world.

ON THE LECTURE CIRCUIT AND SETTING MORE RECORDS

Arriving in New York, she found that George Putnam had arranged a ticker-tape parade. Kids from Denison House attended and called out to her. Putnam set up numerous lectures and suggested she smile with her lips closed so that no one would see the gap between her front teeth. Receptions, marching bands, medals, interviews, and lectures became a

In later years, some of Amelia's work involved promotion of products such as malted milk balls. [Putnam Collection of Amelia Earhart papers]

new part of her life. She received the nickname Lady Lindy because of her resemblance to Charles Lindbergh. She did not like this and later apologized to his wife, Anne Morrow Lindbergh.

Putnam kept Amelia so busy that she had very little time to visit with her family. Once she gave thirty-three talks in twenty-five days. In one year she made 150 appearances. She earned up to $350 per lecture, equal to about $5,000 in today's dollars. She needed a lot of money to keep flying and breaking records, which in turn provided more material for her lectures. "It is sheer, thumping hard work to be a hero," said Putnam.

In the 1920s, people thought this new business of flying was unnatural and dangerous. Women did not fly, and they did not want their husbands to fly, either. Amelia tried to change attitudes about safety, facilities, and fears during her lectures. She explained that because a plane was not connected to the ground, a flight would not make them dizzy like a roller coaster. Because there were no signs or poles to give a sense of speed, the motion seemed slow and "air flowed like liquid" over the plane.

Amelia was asked if women could be the equals of men in aviation. "No, not in aviation," she said. "In everything."

Amelia was appointed aviation editor for *Cosmopolitan* magazine and wrote sixteen articles about the new field. She also worked to start up a commercial airline. While she received bags of fan mail and "Amelia" became a popular name for new babies, she continued to make daring flights and became the first woman to fly solo across the United States from east to west and then back east again.

Meanwhile, her family had many troubles, and Amelia sent clothes and money to her mother and sister, who now had a baby son. Her father was remarried and very ill. Amelia helped with his debts and medical bills and spent a week with him in California just before he died.

George Putnam was her promoter and supporter in all things. He sent her to his house in Rye, New York, with a secretary, and she wrote a bestselling book about the *Friendship* flight titled *20 Hrs. 40 Mins.* In two years he asked her to marry him six times. She finally said yes, and they married in a very simple ceremony in 1931. The

Amelia on a fishing trip with George Putnam (far left) and Fred Noonan.
[Putnam Collection of Amelia Earhart papers]

bride wore brown and wanted no publicity. "Please let us not interfere with the other's work or play," she asked of Putnam, "nor let the world see our private joys or disagreements."

SOLO OVER THE ATLANTIC, 1932

Amelia eventually developed a deep desire to fly solo across the Atlantic Ocean. For this she would need a sturdier and more powerful plane. The little Avian she had bought in England was so light that she could pick it up by the tail and drag it around the field. She had flown it across the country and back, but to race in the first women's transcontinental air derby in 1929, she sold it and bought a used Lockheed Vega.

Amelia flew the used Vega cross-country to prepare for the derby and took it to the Lockheed factory to see whether it needed any adjustments. After Wiley Post, the company's test pilot, took it for a spin, he said the plane was the "foulest he had ever flown." Lockheed officials were so impressed with her ability to fly such a plane that they let her trade it in for a red Lockheed Vega 5B.

After three years flying the red Vega, she decided she had enough experience to try a solo flight over the Atlantic. Amelia had the plane reconditioned and customized in secrecy at Teterboro Airport in New Jersey. She planned to fly from Newfoundland to Paris, France. The wooden fuselage was strengthened, and a 500-horsepower supercharged engine was installed. Extra fuel tanks were added in the wings and cabin, then extra fuses and a hand pump in case the motor-driven fuel pump failed.

A drift indicator, two new compasses, and a directional gyro compass were also added. Amelia was very aware that looking from side to side contributed to pilot fatigue, so the cockpit was designed with everything in easy reach. For a final touch she made a place for a thermos of hot chocolate or canned tomato juice.

While she continued with lectures and answering letters, she also practiced flying blind, using only instruments to determine where she was in the air. She would have to know how to rely on these instruments during black nights, fog, and storms, when she couldn't see out the window. She continued to keep her preparations a secret, even from her family, because other female pilots were also making plans to fly across the Atlantic. Amelia was very aware of the danger and thought her chance of success was "one in ten." Her philosophy was "The time to worry is three months before a flight. Decide then whether or not the goal is worth the risks involved. If it is, stop worrying."

In the third week of May 1932, she flew to Harbour Grace, Newfoundland, but the weather was blustery. Things improved in the evening as the wind blew gently into the face of the plane, a perfect moment for takeoff. She pulled on the throttle and lifted up into the last light of the day.

The moon was glowing, and everything was okay despite the extra weight. But then the altimeter, the instrument to measure altitude, quit working. She was also alarmed to see flames around a broken weld in the engine. Then the moon disappeared behind the clouds, followed by hours of rain and lightning.

Amelia wrote into her log: "If anyone finds the wreck, know that the nonsuccess was caused by my getting lost in a storm for an hour."

She climbed higher to get above the storm, but the wings and windshield iced over. The plane plummeted three thousand feet in a tailspin. She managed to pull it out just before hitting the ocean. Calmly she flew very close to the waves while the ice melted. Then

Amelia in Northern Ireland after a historic solo flight across the Atlantic in 1932.

[Schlesinger Libraries, Radcliffe Institute]

she plowed through fog, tried to switch to a reserve fuel tank, and discovered a fuel line leak. The plan to reach Paris was no longer possible.

Amelia made an emergency landing in Robert Gallagher's cow pasture near Londonderry, Northern Ireland, on May 21, 1932. Her solo flight took fourteen hours, fifty-six minutes, much less than the thirty-three hours, thirty minutes for Charles Lindbergh to reach Paris. Despite rumors, she never killed a cow and had more than one gallon left in the tank because she had to pay Irish taxes on a hundred gallons of fuel. During this record-breaking flight she only sipped a can of tomato juice.

Three months later, she made the first solo, nonstop flight by a woman across the United States, from Los Angeles to Newark, New Jersey. The flight covered 2,447 miles and lasted nineteen hours, fifteen minutes. Eleven months later, she flew the same course and broke her own record in seventeen hours, seven minutes. Amelia became even more famous, gave speeches on aviation and women's rights, and had dinner at the White House with President Herbert Hoover. She was awarded several medals, including a special medal from the National Geographic Society for being the first woman to make a solo transatlantic flight.

After Franklin Roosevelt became president in 1933, she and Putnam often stayed at the White House when they were in town. Amelia became a very good friend of First Lady Eleanor Roosevelt.

On a night flight, Amelia shows Washington, D.C., to First Lady Eleanor Roosevelt.
[Putnam Collection of Amelia Earhart papers]

After a formal dinner, while still dressed in silk evening gowns, Amelia took Eleanor for a ride in a Condor airplane. Eleanor was very interested in flying, got a student permit, and passed the required eye tests. But President Franklin said no, it was too dangerous.

FASHIONABLE AMELIA

In late 1933, Amelia launched a clothing line, Amelia Fashions, for "the woman who lives actively," and sold the garments in New York

DESIGNED BY
Amelia Earhart

Using her own label, Amelia designed sportswear, skirts, dresses, pants, and a two-piece flying suit. She used strong, washable fabrics like parachute silk and Grenfell cotton.

and Chicago. She made her own samples with strong washable materials like Grenfell cotton and parachute silk used in the aviation industry. Details for blouses, pants, suits, and hats included propeller-shaped buttons and other aviation designs.

Amelia was the first person to sell clothing as separates, meaning that the buyer could purchase tops and bottoms in different sizes. To make the clothing more affordable, she also provided patterns for people to make their own clothes. Shirts were made extra long. "I made up my mind," she said, "that if the wearers of the shirts I designed for any reason took time out to stand on their heads, there would *still* be enough shirt to stay tucked in."

The clothing line was meant to help finance her flying, but ultimately it failed. It was launched during the Great Depression, and most people had no extra income for clothes. Many workers were unemployed and standing in breadlines. But still Amelia managed to keep flying.

MORE RECORDS

In 1935, Amelia became the first person, male or female, to fly solo from Honolulu to Oakland, California. Then she was the first to fly from Los Angeles to Mexico City. On the way she got an insect in her eye and ended up landing in a cow pasture. After eight days of reshaping the runway and waiting for better weather, she crossed seven hundred miles of the Gulf of Mexico to finally reach Newark, New Jersey, another record.

When she crossed the gulf in her latest Lockheed Vega with its single Wasp engine, she realized it would be necessary to have a multi-motored plane to make a big ocean crossing. As she continued with lectures, worked to reelect Franklin Roosevelt, remodeled a new house in North Hollywood, and fought off sinus and other health issues, a new plan percolated in her mind. She was yearning for one more great flight—to go all around the world at its "waist," staying very close to the equator. This would be a distance of more than twenty-five thousand miles with big ocean crossings. Could she get the plane she needed to make this happen?

FLIGHT AROUND THE WORLD

Amelia was working with Purdue University in West Lafayette, Indiana, to help build an aviation department. The school had its own landing field and was coed, offering engineering for women as well as men. Amelia always thought that there should be more opportunities for women who liked to "tinker." "Study what you want," she said. "Don't let the world push you around." Female enrollment greatly increased while she was teaching.

Purdue Research Foundation and other donors helped her get a new two-motor Lockheed Electra 10E, a big step up from her single-engine Vega. She got it on her thirty-ninth birthday, July 24, 1936.

Amelia called this new $80,000 plane (about $1.4 million today) a "flying laboratory." It had a Sperry Gyro-Pilot that could fly the ship unaided, a Bendix radio direction finder to locate radio stations, and the finest two-way voice and code communications equipment. It also had all-metal retractable landing gear and a cruising speed of 180 miles per hour.

The ten passenger seats were removed to make room for extra gas tanks to increase the plane's range. The fuel lines were encased in rubber tubing to prevent leaking. The gas tanks took up so much space that a catwalk was built over the top to connect the cockpit with the rear of the plane. Later, to lighten the load, she did not hesitate to remove radio and Morse code equipment and even the parachutes.

This was just the plane Amelia wanted to fly around the world at the equator. Except for the very first leg, she would be the only pilot. Fred Noonan was picked to handle navigation and radio operation. Fred had left home at age fifteen to go to sea and had been on three torpedoed British ships. He had rounded Cape Horn seven times and had a first-class pilot's license on the Mississippi River. Most important, he worked with Pan American World Airways to open up the Pacific Ocean for air travel.

Amelia, with help from her husband, made a plan to circle the world going west, starting in Oakland, California, with the first leg heading to Honolulu, Hawaii. The westward direction was timed to avoid the monsoon season in Asia and major dust storms in Africa.

From Honolulu she would make a long sixty-five-hundred-mile hop to tiny Howland Island in the middle of the Pacific Ocean. This speck of land, a half degree north of the equator and only two miles by one mile, would be very hard to find. The island had no people but millions of seabirds. Since it didn't have a runway, President Roosevelt decided to have one built there in a hurry.

George Putnam spent a month going from embassy to embassy in Washington, D.C., seeking permission from countries on five continents to land and fly in their airspace. Amelia studied which airports

Amelia poses with Fred Noonan and a map of the route over the Pacific Ocean.
[Putnam Collection of Amelia Earhart papers]

in remote places would have adequate runways, refueling, and repair facilities. They spent long days writing letters, studying charts and weather reports, calculating fuel supplies, and deciding where to stock-pile extra fuel and when to send engineers to faraway airports with spare parts.

On March 17, 1937, Amelia began the westward round-the-world adventure at the airport in Oakland. Workers there made a special seven-thousand-foot runway for the Electra. Navigator Fred Noonan, Paul Mantz, who oversaw the plane reconditioning, and Captain Harry Manning were on this first leg as "extra eyes" to evaluate all systems. They used a cut-down bamboo fishing pole with an office clip to hold messages between the pilot and navigator. They landed in rec-ord time: Oakland to Honolulu in fifteen hours, fifty-two minutes.

The next hop would be tiny Howland Island, and Amelia refueled with extra gasoline to reach it or return to Hawaii if necessary. There was a big push to finish the island's primitive runway. After a week of delays and heavy rain, conditions were right to head off for that little speck in the vast Pacific Ocean. This attempt was likened to flying cross-country from Los Angeles in complete fog with no recognizable landmarks, hoping to find the eighteenth hole on a New Jersey golf course.

The first step was the takeoff, which quickly turned to disaster as a tire blew on the concrete runway and maybe the right shock absorber failed. As the wing dropped and the plane pulled to the right, Amelia reduced the power. But with excessive weight from extra fuel, the right

The Lockheed Electra crashed in Honolulu in the first attempt to reach Howland Island.

[Putnam Collection of Amelia Earhart papers]

landing gear pulled free and gasoline sprayed out. Amelia kept calm and quickly turned off the engine. There was no fire or explosion, and everyone exited the metal plane safely. But with collapsed landing gear and a torn wing, the flight ended. The Electra was hoisted onto a boat and made a slow sea journey back to Oakland.

PLAN B

Many thought that Amelia might quit, but she did not. Her mother would later write that Amelia always "considered the plane she used as if it were a living creature. It was like a favorite pony. We said good-night to it and petted its nose and almost fed it apples. The last plane . . . was the one we were especially attached to." One story says that this favorite plane was redesigned, rebuilt, and retested to be declared airworthy. However, another version states that the plane was secretly replaced by a similar but advanced model, the Electra 12. This advanced model was then outfitted with two Fairchild aerial surveillance cameras in its belly. Were these added to take photos of Japanese activity in the Marshall Islands? Japan had possession of these Pacific islands but was not allowed to add runways or military installations. As tensions built up before World War II, President Roosevelt would want to know if the Japanese were doing anything illegal.

As she waited almost three months for a plane, Amelia secretly reversed the direction of the adventure. This time she intended to start in Miami and go east. New letters were written to change permissions, visas, and dates set up with foreign airports. This was a serious financial commitment. It included details such as paying an aviation expert who had traveled from London to India to deliver parts and service the plane. He had to return home, and they hoped he'd be available again when it was time to fly.

While Amelia and her husband took care of details, Amelia received many letters from kids and adults. *Amelia* was becoming the most popular name for newborn girls, pets, and even the fastest-flying pigeon in Florida. One little girl said, "I would have named my duck Amelia but since it is a he duck I can't." Another child wrote, "Please teach me to fly. . . . I will repay you if it takes the rest of my life. . . . I haven't got much because my father loads coal in a mine." She did hear some criticism, though. After she had taken off for Honolulu in March, a prominent newspaperman in Kansas exhorted her, "In the long lone watches over the gray and melancholy ocean, comb your head, kid, comb your head!"

Paul Mantz, who usually oversaw plane details, was not involved in the second attempt of the world flight. He was unhappy to hear that Amelia had removed a heavy 250-foot trailing radio antenna because she didn't like to reel it out and back in again. However, if she had a new plane with much better radio equipment, this long antenna wouldn't be needed.

Amelia and Fred started the second journey from Miami on June 1, 1937. This event was witnessed by only a small group because

Amelia kept most details a secret, even from her family. Right after takeoff, a Miami radio station broadcast a news flash. Amelia was back in the air! The news made headlines around the world.

Amelia and Fred flew off to Puerto Rico and then on to Caripito, Venezuela, where Amelia marveled at the lush orchids at her dining table. From there, they headed to Paramaribo, the capital of Dutch Guiana (now Suriname). Amelia was pleased to discover that the airport was very prepared with an orange wind sock, white flags, and a bonfire to guide them. They refueled the tanks and greased the propellers before taking off again, making two stops in Brazil. After that there were stops across northern Africa as they made their way to India, their fourth continent.

Everywhere people followed the logbooks, notes, and radio news about the adventure. Amelia wrote that she liked the jungle in Venezuela, that the Red Sea looked blue, and that the Arabian shore was desolate. She was sorry that they had no time to see the sights until they had a two-day layover in Karachi. There she rode a camel and visited an oasis. She sent back photos and notes and told her husband that she was "swell. Never better."

They had their difficulties. Because they flew through an area with yellow fever, the plane had to be sprayed with insecticide whenever they landed. They had a terrible time with monsoons as they tried to get to Bangkok. After a refueling stop in Akyab, Burma (now Sittwe, Myanmar), a deluge forced them to turn around and spend the night there. Even more rain prompted an unscheduled overnight in Rangoon, now known as Yangon. After two days of scheduled maintenance in Bandung, Java, they had to return for more work before proceeding to Timor, Indonesia, and on to Darwin, Australia.

Finally, on June 29, they reached Lae, New Guinea. They loaded up with extra fuel and took off on July 2, 1937, for the long flight to find tiny Howland Island.

To help them locate the landing spot, the Coast Guard cutter *Itasca* was stationed near the island with radios and lights blaring and black smoke billowing, ready to scare off huge flocks of terns, frigates, and albatrosses that might be on the runway when the Electra arrived for touchdown. About midway between Lae and the island, navy personnel on the *Ontario* were prepared to help if they received a distress signal from the plane. Unfortunately, communication problems developed, and messages from Amelia were garbled. For two and a half hours they heard nothing from her at all. They never saw her fly overhead. Was she lost? Was she down to her last drop of fuel?

A weak message gave a clue about the line of flight that she was following. But was she going north or south along this line? Was that storm in the north blowing her off course?

As the day wore on, there were no more communications from the Electra.

The headlines now read EARHART PLANE DOWN, LADY LINDY LOST, AE MISSES ISLAND ON LONG HOP.

The world flight became the last flight as Amelia Earhart disappeared.

A map of Amelia's attempted flight around the world.

SEARCHING FOR AMELIA

Sorrow and disbelief were felt around the world. Admiral William D. Leahy, chief of naval operations, ordered that all practicable naval facilities be used in the search for Amelia and Fred. The aircraft carrier *Lexington*, the battleship *Colorado*, four destroyers, and a minesweeper searched 262,281 square miles of the Pacific Ocean, with shore parties going to tiny islands. At a cost of $4.9 million ($83.3 million today), this was the greatest air-and-sea search in history. They found no plane parts, no sign of survivors, not even a drop of oil.

The U.S. government asked permission from the Japanese to search the Marshall Islands, but they refused. The Japanese said they would conduct a search with several vessels in the area, including a plane tender and huge aircraft carrier.

Finally, George Putnam financed a private search, chartering boats to explore the Phoenix Islands, the Gilbert Islands, and other possible landing areas. They found nothing.

Hundreds of letters came addressed to "Mother of Amelia Earhart, California, U.S.A." One letter was from a woman who saw Amelia after her first crossing of the Atlantic in 1928. "I recognized her as an ideal of so many young women who dream but do not dare to do the pioneering." Amelia's mother kept a suitcase packed in the hope that her daughter would be found and she could fly to her. Eleanor Roosevelt chaired a group that intended to conduct a search.

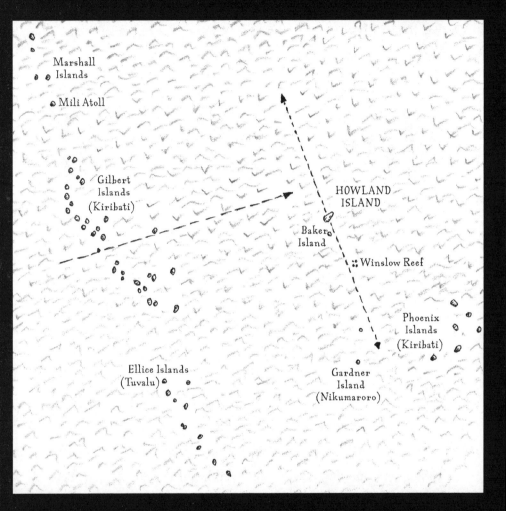

Map of search area. Amelia called in a line of flight (dotted lines), but did she go south toward Gardner Island? Or did she go north? If she ended up at Mili Atoll, were the Marshall Islands her real destination? Or did she crash and disappear in a vast ocean?

Finally, without a single crash clue or a sign of survivors, Amelia Earhart was declared legally dead on January 5, 1939. Fred Noonan had been declared dead on June 20, 1938, because his widow wanted to remarry and had petitioned a court for a resolution.

THE SEARCH GOES ON AND ON AND ON . . .

This did not end the search. Numerous theories, books, and articles have been written about the fate of Amelia Earhart and Fred Noonan.

One theory is that Amelia ran out of fuel, crashed, and sank into the ocean. Through the years a large area of ocean around Howland Island has been mapped and searched by towed submersibles. Teams with sonar have combed through this area numerous times, but no airplane parts or other artifacts that can be absolutely identified have been found.

Radio buffs reported hearing messages from Amelia for several days after she was due at Howland Island. Some of these were hoaxes, but others are harder to ignore. Garbled messages indicated that Noonan was injured, and they needed help. Did the plane end up on a remote island that everyone missed? If so, where was it?

One point of focus has taken searchers south to Gardner Island, now called Nikumaroro. Ric Gillespie, head of a group called TIGHAR (the International Group for Historic Aircraft Recovery), believes that the plane landed there on a reef. Then Amelia made radio broadcasts for five nights by running the engine to charge the batteries.

However, this island was searched by navy planes back in 1937, and they never saw Amelia or the plane. Gillespie has made numerous trips to this island and found various items such as a rusted pocketknife, bottles, zippers, pieces of a shoe, and an aluminum sheet with rivets. People lived on the island between 1939 and 1963, and these items could have belonged to them. None of these clues can be directly connected to Amelia.

Books have been written about Amelia living in New Jersey under the name Irene Craigmile Bolam. This story started in 1965, when a retired pilot saw Bolam and thought she was Amelia. Many facts of her life showed that Irene could not be Amelia. Bolam sued the publisher, and the book was withdrawn. However, this was not the end of books and speculation about Amelia in New Jersey.

A high school teacher named Dick Spink was visiting the Marshall Islands when he heard stories from the Marshallese about a female pilot and a man who had landed there and were picked up by the Japanese. He has spent over $50,000 of his own money making several excursions to search Mili Atoll, about nine hundred miles northwest of Howland Island. On the atoll's tiny Endriken Island he found several pieces from an airplane that could possibly be from the Electra. The proof is not absolute, but he and others feel that these pieces tie

The arrow points to tiny Endriken Island, part of Mili Atoll in the Marshall Islands. Metal airplane parts were found here. Possibly the Electra crashed in the vicinity. [Dick Spink]

into stories that Amelia and Fred crashed on Endriken and were picked up by the Japanese.

Interviews with older residents of the Marshall Islands indicated that a slender woman with short hair and an injured man had landed there and that an airplane had been loaded on a barge. Since the original witnesses are now dead, others are passing along their stories. One possible scenario came from Bilimon Amaron, a Marshallese who was a medic in the Japanese navy. He said he had treated a white man with a head wound and a serious leg injury.

The stories are intriguing but not consistent. For instance, some say Amelia died of dysentery in a Japanese prison in Saipan. Another story is that she was pushed into a grave. Fred may have been beheaded. The airplane may have been buried, maybe both wings were removed, or perhaps it was completely destroyed?

What was she doing up in the Marshall Islands, hundreds of miles off course? Was she lost? Windblown? Or did she agree to photograph the extent of Japanese occupation in these tiny islands? A recently discovered photograph meant to prove her presence in the Marshall Islands turned out to have been taken two years before she arrived.

The mystery of her disappearance is still not solved.

But all remember that Amelia Earhart inspired women to do things that once only men would do. That she was full of energy and new ideas and would never quit. Amelia Earhart taught the world about being a pioneer and doing "first time things."

CHAPTER 5

William Morgan and a Book of Secrets

Carriage driving off with William Morgan.

IN WESTERN NEW YORK STATE, a crisis roiled in September 1826. It was fueled with fear and paranoia and a book of secrets. Would it end in murder?

Several men in Batavia, New York, were trying to convince William Morgan to never publish his completed manuscript. The book threatened to reveal secrets that they had all sworn to keep—hand

William Morgan had once been a storekeeper, a bricklayer, and a stonecutter, but he ran into real trouble when he decided to publish a book. [Library of Congress]

signs and door knocks, costumes and ceremonies, symbols and word phrases.

It all started when publisher David C. Miller announced in his *Republican Advocate* newspaper that he would publish Morgan's illustrated book, which would bring everything to light that had been concealed by the fraternity these men belonged to. The men responded first by running an ad calling Morgan a "most undesirable character" and organizing a boycott of the newspaper.

Soon after, several dozen men got riled up and decided to burn down the newspaper offices. Miller managed to put out the fire. Then they had Morgan arrested for owing money. While Morgan was imprisoned over a weekend, they went to his home, pushed past his wife, and searched for the manuscript. They had no luck.

On Monday, Miller was able to pay off the alleged debt and get Morgan out of jail. However, Morgan was quickly accused of stealing a shirt and tie and returned to jail. Miller was also arrested and intimidated by several men but then released without charges.

On September 13, Loton Lawson, a farmer whom Morgan did not know, paid for Morgan's release. Once Morgan was freed, Lawson urged him to get into his yellow carriage. Morgan refused. Two other men showed up. "Murder!" yelled Morgan as the men shoved him into the carriage and clattered off down the road.

Lawson and others had a plan to take Morgan to Fort Niagara on Lake Ontario and the mouth of the Niagara River. In those rough times of frontier traveling, two days were required for a 120-mile journey. They regularly stopped to water the horses and get fresh ones. Twice they changed carriages. Along the way they were joined by Eli Bruce, the sheriff of Niagara County.

There were no troops at the fort when they arrived. According to

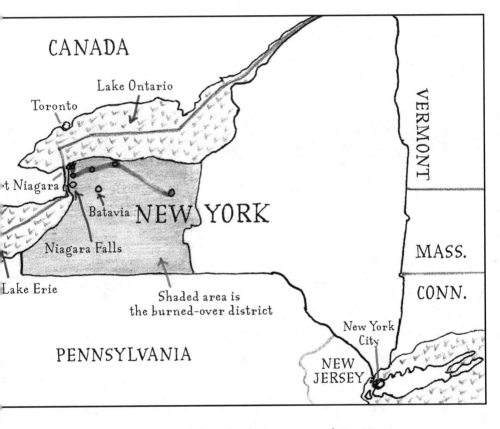

The kidnappers needed two days by carriage to reach Fort Niagara.

court testimony, lighthouse keeper Edward Giddings had the keys to a storehouse in the fort, and he allowed them to imprison Morgan there. After the men found a boat, they crossed the river with their captive and urged him to disappear into the Canadian wilderness and not publish the book. Morgan refused. They brought him back to the fort and gave him very little food or water. Now what? A captive author was a gigantic problem. How desperate were they?

In the far outreaches of a rugged frontier, only this much was certain: William Morgan was missing.

CROSSING OUT A NAME

The kidnappers were Freemasons. William Morgan was also a Freemason, regarded as clever, but also quarrelsome and dishonest. Morgan had signed a petition for a new lodge to be built in a nearby village. However, some in Batavia were unwilling to have Morgan as a member. A line was drawn through his name, and William Morgan became an angry ex-Freemason. He had debts, a wife, and two kids. He would now be denied charity from this group. Would he also be denied a job in the new construction? William Morgan had good writing skills, a great memory, and an ability to make woodcuts. He decided to write a tell-all book about the Freemasons. It could lead to fame and fortune.

The kidnappers meant to prevent that. When they were caught, they claimed to have offered Morgan $500 to disappear across the border. But did he? Or did the captors drown him in the Niagara River, as later testimony and deathbed confessions implied?

David C. Miller didn't wait for Morgan's return or for his body to show up. He printed Morgan's book, *Illustrations of Masonry*, and sold copies for $1. The local scandal quickly became big news everywhere. With all the hoopla, the book became a bestseller.

It was not the first book to reveal secrets. In England there were numerous such books. In 1730, Samuel Prichard wrote *Masonry Dissected*, which explained the three degrees of initiation. It went through eleven printings in eleven days and remained in print for over thirty years. Masons often bought it as a memory aid. William Preston's *Illustrations of Masonry*, in 1772, went through twelve editions in the author's lifetime. Some editions of these or similar books may have been available in the colonies. But in 1826, out on the frontier, did Morgan know this? Did anyone know this? These were the same secrets, revealed over and over again.

In William Morgan's neighborhood, fiery religious revivals were conducted in every village. The region was known as the "burned-over district," where fundamentalist preachers and others encouraged suspicion of secretive societies as immoral, unchristian, and undemocratic. The abduction of William Morgan by Freemasons aroused a dormant hostility against this secretive society. Much of the public turned completely against the Freemasons, even though almost all members had nothing to do with this tragic moment.

Timothy Flint, editor of the *Western Monthly Review* of October 1829, wrote, "A small number of foolish and misguided men, under wild and mistaken notions of masonic responsibility, carried off a certain Mr. Morgan, leaving the natural inference from his disappearance." There was no body, but most thought that William Morgan had been murdered.

Many Freemasons were accused of involvement, and several trials were held in five counties. Most of the prosecutors, sheriffs, judges, and juries involved were Freemasons. The many long trials dominated the national news. When the kidnappers received very light sentences, growing suspicions about the fraternity exploded into a national outrage. Were the Freemasons protecting each other? Was this secret society powerful enough to establish its own system of justice and punishment?

Some citizens became determined to see the total destruction of the secretive group. They started an Anti-Masonic religious movement that raged through the burned-over district and beyond. All that frenzy became a political party called the Anti-Masons. In the end, the disappearance of William Morgan led to the interruption of free speech and the right to gather. It also led to innovative changes in the political and judicial systems of the United States.

SO WHAT'S A FREEMASON, AND WHY KEEP SECRETS?

Long ago, master craftsmen built stone cathedrals, stone castles, stone towers, stone bridges, stone monasteries, and other structures that have endured for centuries.

The craftsmen worked at two levels. The rough masons used hard stone to build foundations. Then highly skilled artisans came in with soft chalky stone, called freestone, which could be scraped and shaped into wonderful designs. They were called freestone masons, or freemasons for short.

Freemasons were paid by kings, queens, and archbishops in the Middle Ages and traveled all over England, Scotland, France, and other countries to build beautiful, inspiring stone structures. They led lives very different from the serfs and local craftsmen who were tied to one place. Freemasons were away from home for months on end, so they built huts, called lodges, as places to share meals and store their chisels, levels, compasses, and other tools.

They were similar to guilds for other trades such as roofers, carpenters, rope makers, hatters, and smiths. The Freemasons used the security of their lodges to draw up building plans based on the geometry of squares and triangles. Like other craftsmen, the stone workers kept their methods a secret. Even the kings and bishops who hired

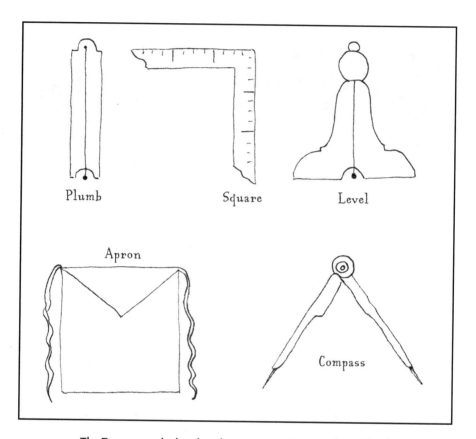

The Freemasons had tools to keep construction straight and level.

them did not know how they transformed geometric designs into great Gothic structures.

After a terrible plague swept through England in 1348, killing up to one half of the London population, the skills of surviving Freemasons were in great demand. They managed to make illegal agreements to get a higher pay rate than what was allowed by English law.

Early members went through three degrees of initiation. The first ceremony was for entered apprentices. After several years they were made fellow craftsmen. In the third ceremony, they became master masons. They created specific handshakes, passwords, and knocks so that only Freemasons who had gone through the initiation ceremonies could gain entry into a lodge. These methods protected information about their craft and how much they were paid. Also, in a time when

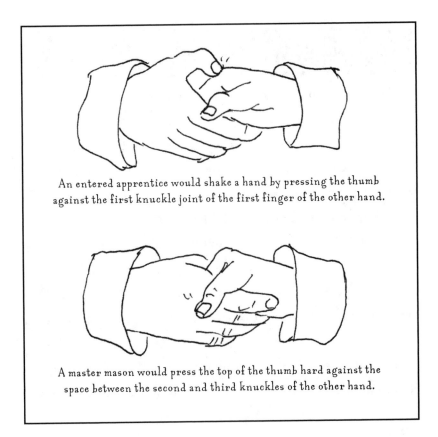

An entered apprentice would shake a hand by pressing the thumb against the first knuckle joint of the first finger of the other hand.

A master mason would press the top of the thumb hard against the space between the second and third knuckles of the other hand.

most craftsmen were illiterate, the secret signs learned at each level allowed them to go from one lodge to another with instant recognition of ability. They just had to use the correct knock and handclasp. Early English records of handshakes, hand signals, and passwords were recorded in the fourteenth century. At a meeting, however, various symbols might be drawn on the floor with chalk or coal and then erased with a mop.

CHANGE COMES TO THE FREEMASONS

William Morgan became a Freemason after his failed attempt to run a brewery in Canada, which burned to the ground. He ended up in western New York as a stonemason and joined the Freemasons in the 1820s. Numerous officials in the area were members, and sixteen of twenty-two townships had lodges. They were a big part of rural life. But over the centuries, many things had changed.

As the Middle Ages passed into the Renaissance and then to the Age of Reason, men began to value science and artistry. The invention of the printing press allowed people to read more books, but there was much religious persecution that made people fear for their lives.

In the 1500s and 1600s, religious wars raged throughout Europe. For instance, under Charles II, England was officially Protestant, but the next king, James II, insisted that all his subjects become Catholics. With every new ruler, subjects had to wonder which Bible to read. Was it now safe to say this or that? Careless speech or new inventions could lead to prison, torture, and death. Inventors could be convicted of heresy by coming up with an idea that did not agree with the beliefs of the church. For instance, Galileo Galilei used his telescope to study the stars and planets and wrote articles about his belief that the earth revolved around the sun. The Catholic Church believed that everything revolved around the earth and sentenced Galileo to life imprisonment in 1633.

Change came to the stonemasons, too, as bricks became the new building material. The Freemasons, sometimes called the Masons, were losing work and losing members. However, the secrecy of the lodge began to appeal to people who didn't know a thing about carving a gargoyle or making a turret. Could a lodge provide a meeting place where an idea, any idea, might be discussed without fear of torture or beheading? Many wanted to model their ideas on scientific method rather than on religious dogma, magic, or superstition. The action of joining with builders became symbolic of "building" new ideas and philosophies and "bridging" friendships to new people.

Four lodges in London felt that a governing lodge was needed to keep the Masonic structure uniform as the group attracted new members. They wanted each lodge to have similar songs, costumes, rituals, and furniture. By this point, Freemasons were meeting in public houses,

At the Goose and Gridiron alehouse,
the upstairs rooms provided space and privacy.

inns, and taverns, and lodges took their name from where they met. In 1717, the Goose and Gridiron alehouse in Saint Paul's churchyard hosted a joint meeting with members from the Crown alehouse in Parker's Lane, the Apple Tree Tavern in Charles Street, and the Rummer and Grapes tavern in Channel Row. The four decided to form a Grand Lodge, which would have authority over all lodges in England.

The original Freemasons decided to allow other craftsmen and noncraftsmen to join. They were delighted to find that doctors, lawyers, educators, and craftsmen such as hatters and blacksmiths wanted to meet in a protected lodge. They were eventually surprised when the Prince of Wales joined, as later would his sons, the Duke of Gloucester, the Duke of Cumberland, and the Duke of York, the brothers of King George III. A lodge became a place where the aristocratic class could mix with others, something that would normally not be allowed in society.

In a lodge, people of all religions were accepted, including Catholics, Anglicans, Presbyterians, Calvinists, Puritans, and Jews. As travelers ventured to and from the Far East, Buddhists, Muslims, and followers of Confucius joined. Members tolerated and looked for understanding of different religious views. Religion and politics, however, were not discussed in a lodge. Instead members pursued science and invention with no censorship from any church or ruling king. They were encouraged to become the best people they could be.

Charitable work was also part of the activities. Freemasons supported each other and their relatives, but they were also involved with "the prisoner, the widow, the orphan and the poor . . . the relief of human misery," according to Timothy Flint.

One important leader was John Theophilus Desaguliers. His father, a Protestant pastor, had been forced to flee religious intolerance in France. He left behind his pregnant wife, who gave birth to a baby boy in 1683. She and the baby, John, soon followed her husband

Mrs. Aldworth, from Ireland, became a Freemason in 1710. She overheard a ritual and was urged to join as a good way to keep the secret. [Library of Congress]

to England, in secret because France required that Protestant children be left behind to be educated as Roman Catholics. Some stories say she hid him in a barrel as they crossed the sea.

When John grew up, he joined the Freemasons and worked with Isaac Newton, one of the most influential scientists ever, studying gravity, tides, and comets, among other subjects. John studied many theories of his own and also became quite interested in Freemasonry as a good way to advance religious tolerance. He had no trouble

persuading friends in the aristocracy to join the society and was chosen as the third grand master in the new Grand Lodge.

By 1735, the number of new lodges in England had grown to 126.
Gradually other Grand Lodges were formed, with satellite lodges all
over Europe and eventually most of the world. Each language and
culture brought a few changes, but the main idea was always appar-
ent: All members were to make themselves better and to treat others
as they would want to be treated. In England, women were usually
not allowed to join, just as they could not be professors, lawyers, ju-
rists, and a host of other positions. In France, however, women were
admitted after the eighteenth century. Empress Josephine, the wife of
Napoleon, presided when a Freemason lodge held an initiation in
Strasbourg, France.

The poet Goethe, the author Voltaire, the philosopher John
Locke, and the statesman Benjamin Franklin were drawn to the fraternity. Musicians were especially interested. Franz Joseph Haydn was a
member, and Wolfgang Amadeus Mozart joined in 1784. Mozart
was so influenced that most of his music was written with the Freemasons in mind. He was employed by an archbishop who paid him
poorly and treated him like a member of the kitchen staff. But when
Mozart became a Freemason, he received respect, and creative notes
flowed from that relationship. This included music for the opening
and closing of a lodge, and the opera *The Magic Flute*. The purpose of his
Masonic music was to spread good thoughts, unity, joy, and loyalty,

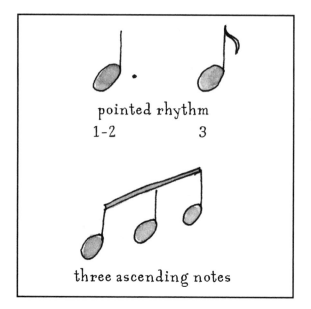

pointed rhythm
1-2   3

three ascending notes

Three is an important number in a lodge, and there are references to three burning tapers, three knocks, three guides, and three pillars. Mozart wrote thirteen lodge songs, often using chords, flats, and rhythms related to three.

all important feelings for this growing society. Because the number three was important, with three initiations, three steps up to the grand master's chair, and three pillars, he often used three notes together to represent this connection.

Not everyone was happy with this secretive organization that accepted all religions. In 1738, Pope Clement XII banned church members from joining, with consequences such as the rack, a large fine in gold, or years as a galley slave. At least eight other popes also issued

George Washington in Masonic clothes. He wore these items to Masonic meetings and some public ceremonies, which kept a link to the stonemasons of the Middle Ages.

[Library of Congress]

bans. Any church that viewed itself as the one and only religion did not care for the Freemasons. Monarchies that feared challenges to their authority also objected. And because the Freemasons had secrets, many people regarded the fraternity with deep suspicion. Just what were they doing behind those closed doors?

FREEMASONS IN THE UNITED STATES

Before William Morgan, or any other colonist, could sign up and learn the ceremonies and symbols, the fraternity had to find its way to America.

Benjamin Franklin joined St. John's lodge in Philadelphia in 1731 and became the grand master in 1734. He printed a book, *The Constitutions of the Freemasons*, that was very influential throughout the thirteen colonies. Joining the Masons were people in commerce, farming, smithing, and manufacturing.

George Washington joined, as did many other famous revolutionaries, including Paul Revere, the Marquis de Lafayette, John Hancock, James Madison, James Monroe, and John Paul Jones. Some people became suspicious, imagining that the revolution had been hatched in the secrecy of a Freemason lodge.

However, many people involved in the American Revolution were not Freemasons, including Patrick Henry, Thomas Jefferson, John Adams, Alexander Hamilton, Thomas Paine, and Nathan Hale.

Benedict Arnold had been a member, but his name was crossed out when he went over to the British. Some Freemasons were British and

Joseph Brant, a Mohawk chief, was also called Thayendanegea, or He Places Together Two Bets. He became a Freemason in London.
[National Anthropological Archives, Smithsonian Institution]

supported George III, ruler of the British kingdom during the American Revolutionary War.

Of the fifty-six men who signed the Declaration of Independence, at least eight were Freemasons. Of the thirty-nine men who approved the Constitution of the United States in 1787, thirteen were, or became, members. Only three were Freemasons before the outbreak of the revolution in 1775.

There were advantages during wartime to being a Freemason. For instance, military lodges were set up that moved around with regiments for both the British and revolutionary armies. Some freed slaves were allowed into military lodges when they joined with the British forces. For either side a lodge became a place to make new contacts, which also might provide lifesaving advantages.

In 1776, Joseph Brant, a Mohawk chief who had fought with the British in the French and Indian War, became a Freemason in London. He returned to America to recruit other Mohawks to fight against the Americans under the British colonel John Butler, a Freemason in a British military lodge in New York. The Mohawks captured several revolutionaries. One story concerns a soldier named McKinstry who was tied to a tree and awaited a tragic fate. He gave a Masonic recognition sign. Brant saw it and ordered McKinstry to be freed.

Similar stories were told when Lieutenant Jonathan Maynard was captured by Brant on May 30, 1778, and again with Captain John Wood on July 22, 1779. They both showed a Masonic sign, and Brant ordered the Mohawks to set them free.

A TRIAL WITHOUT A BODY

After William Morgan disappeared in the yellow carriage, people began to look for him, dead or alive.

In Batavia, Morgan's family raised questions. A committee of nine started an investigation, and Governor Clinton offered a $2,000 reward, then $5,000, for help. They were able to trace the route to Fort Niagara, where boats were hired to rake the riverbed and also the shoreline of Lake Ontario. Eventually a body was found in very poor condition. It was initially identified as William Morgan, even though the size, clothes, and hair were all wrong. But the mood of the citizens was irate. They were already suspicious of this secretive group, and now look at what they had done. Murder!

When Morgan's wife saw the body, she said that it was not her husband. However, because of some similarities with the teeth, she was persuaded to change her mind. In order to charge anyone with murder, a body was needed, and this would have to do.

The body was eventually identified by a grieving Canadian widow who said the hand-sewn clothing belonged to her husband, Timothy Monroe, who had been trying to cross the icy river. This didn't seem to make much difference. "The cry of vengeance against the masons was now on the breeze, and the ghost of Morgan was said to walk," wrote Timothy Flint.

Meanwhile, culprits were identified, with dozens of Freemasons suspected of involvement in the affair. In the end only five men were convicted, and the sheriff got the heaviest sentence of two years, four months. Loton Lawson was sentenced to one year, and others received similar light penalties.

Among the prosecutors, sheriffs, judges, and juries were a number of Freemasons. Many wondered how much the culprits were protected by this secret society! The William Morgan affair was a national scandal. At that time kidnapping was a misdemeanor in New York, but soon the law was changed to make it a felony, with a three-to-fourteen-year sentence of hard labor.

The lighthouse keeper, Edward Giddings, also a Freemason, confessed to locking up William Morgan, and then "after a few days a committee of masons, with himself, delivered over the prisoners to the Canada masons and he was taken over the river and there murdered," according to author A. P. Bentley. Giddings was not allowed to make a sworn statement, however, because he was a skeptic, or an atheist. In those days, atheists were not allowed to testify.

As the trial continued, several confessions and other stories emerged. In one Quaker story, William Morgan was working on his book and was surprised by someone plummeting down his chimney in a cloud of soot. The man then used a cable to pull the writer up the chimney and to the roof. A balloon with a small steam engine awaited. It carried William Morgan and three conspirators off to Niagara Falls.

Meanwhile, outright hostility toward the Freemasons ballooned into an Anti-Masonic movement. In March 1827, the Anti-Masons stirred up huge support against all secret societies. Many felt that more wicked things like the murder of William Morgan would occur again. Some angry citizens wanted to completely destroy the Freemasons.

In western New York, pastors were fired and church members who belonged to the Freemasons were expelled. Freemasons were no longer allowed to serve on juries. Members were pushed, shoved, shunned, and fired from their work. Some said it had a feel similar to what caused pagans to persecute Christians, Catholics to persecute Protestants, Episcopalians to persecute Puritans, and Puritans to persecute Quakers.

As the hostility built into a frenzy, most lodges closed down and returned their charters, jewels, furniture, and costumes to their Grand Lodge. Some groups, however, hung on to these items and went underground, expecting that their benevolent and respected society would soon return to public favor.

ANTI-MASONIC POLITICS

As news of William Morgan's abduction and the subsequent trials spread everywhere, the Anti-Masons expanded into a political movement against slavery and drinking alcohol as well.

John Quincy Adams, the sixth president of the United States, belonged to
several political parties, including the Democratic-Republican, the National
Republican, the Anti-Masonic, and the Whig Parties.
[Library of Congress]

In 1825, John Quincy Adams was elected as the sixth president
of the United States after he defeated Andrew Jackson in a vote by
the House of Representatives. Although Jackson had won the most
votes in the electoral college, he did not have the number required
by the Constitution, and so the decision fell to the House. Jackson

Thurlow Weed, a New York newspaper publisher, became a leading voice for the new Anti-Masonic Party. [Library of Congress]

was furious and won by a landslide when Adams ran for a second term. Jackson was a slave owner and very popular in the southern states, where agriculture was predominant and slavery a way of life. Losing the election left Adams to think about retirement and leisurely days of gardening.

But as the Anti-Mason movement gained momentum, Adams got very involved in politics again. He did not care for Andrew Jackson, his proslavery stance, and his forced removal of American Indians from their homes east of the Mississippi River to places west. He also did not care for Freemasonry and wanted to expose what he saw as its inherent falsehoods. "It is wrong—essentially wrong—a seed of evil, which can never produce any good," he wrote. This sentiment would be predominant in his 1847 book *Letters on the Masonic Institution.*

John Quincy Adams helped to build up the Anti-Mason cause into the first official third party in the United States, the Anti-Masonic Party. Thurlow Weed, a strong supporter of Adams, started a newspaper called the *Anti-Masonic Enquirer.* The paper became the voice for the Anti-Mason movement in New York as he wrote articles to arouse passion again the Freemasons. He felt that they, and all secret societies, were against free government. Since Andrew Jackson was a grand master of his lodge in Tennessee, it was hoped that the fervor against Freemasons from the William Morgan affair could be used to defeat him.

By 1829, many more newspapers were dedicated to the Anti-Mason cause. The party embraced antislavery teetotalers as well as champions of women's rights. It also supported a tariff that would protect the sales price of manufactured goods, which was opposed by Jackson and the southern farmers.

As an Anti-Mason, Thurlow Weed was elected to the New York State Assembly in 1829. The next year in Massachusetts, John Quincy Adams was elected with Anti-Masonic support to the House of Representatives. He received nearly three-quarters of the votes. The new party's candidates won elections across the northern states.

The Freemasons, who usually remained uninvolved, decided to

fight back. They entered politics, wrote letters, and made speeches. Resolutions were passed "disavowing all connection or sympathy with the outrage on Morgan, and claiming that a whole great Fraternity should not be held responsible for the unauthorized and unmasonic acts of a few misguided men," according to Robert Freke Gould, writing in *Library of Freemasonry, Volume 4*. However, they did not expel any members who had been involved in the William Morgan affair.

Masonic work almost ceased for a time, in some places for years. About four hundred lodges in New York State, or two-thirds of the total number, suspended work or became extinct. In Pennsylvania, only forty-six lodges remained active where there had been hundreds. In Vermont, the number of lodges was reduced to zero.

At the national level, the Anti-Masonic Party held a convention in Philadelphia on September 11, 1830, to commemorate the fourth anniversary of the Morgan affair. At that time, the party elected national officers and agreed to nominate a candidate for president the next year at a second convention in Baltimore. In Baltimore, they selected William Wirt. He had been attorney general for Presidents James Monroe and John Quincy Adams, a twelve-year run that was the longest ever for an attorney general.

Wirt had lately represented the Cherokees before the Supreme Court in their effort to keep their land. In *Cherokee Nation v. Georgia*, Wirt argued that the "the Cherokee Nation [was] a foreign nation in the sense of our constitution and law" and was not subject to Georgia's

John Ross, a Cherokee chief, asked William Wirt to represent his tribe
as they were being forced out of their homeland. [Library of Congress]

jurisdiction. He lost, but the court reversed itself a year later and
agreed with his argument in *Worcester v. Georgia*. Georgia, however,
ignored the ruling, and neither the court nor President Jackson
enforced it. This eventually led to the Trail of Tears, a series of forced
relocations of the Cherokees and other tribes.

William Wirt was a reluctant candidate for president for
the Anti-Masonic party. [Library of Congress]

Before the choice of William Wirt, presidential candidates had
been selected by a party's caucus in Congress. The Anti-Masons
innovated the first-ever national nominating convention for a political
party. Wirt, like John Quincy Adams, was hoping for an electoral
alliance between the Anti-Masons and the National Republicans to
defeat President Jackson, a Democrat. However, Wirt was a former
Freemason and a very reluctant candidate. He later admitted, "In
the canvass I took no part, not even by writing private letters."

The Anti-Masonic Party also held meetings to decide on the party platform, the ideas that members thought important. This was another first in political history. The two other parties liked these innovations and soon held nominating and platform gatherings of their own.

When the elections were held, Democratic incumbent President Jackson easily won reelection, defeating Henry Clay of the National Republican Party, William Wirt, and Independent John Floyd. Jackson won 219 of the 286 electoral votes. William Wirt received 100,715 votes, only 7.8 percent of the total, and seven electoral votes from Vermont.

After this huge defeat, most Anti-Masons switched to the new anti-Jackson coalition, the Whig Party. Issues to consider included Arkansas, which wanted to be admitted to the union with a constitution that prevented its legislature from ever "giving freedom to the slave." In 1835, there were antiabolitionist riots in New York and Baltimore, and a number of abolitionists were hanged for circulating antislavery literature. John Quincy Adams continued as a member of the House, working hard against slavery.

Interest in defeating Freemasonry waned as antislavery became the big concern. Lodge membership rebounded during the late 1830s as the fraternity became popular again. It took many years of conflict before the slavery issue had to be settled with the Civil War. During the war, lodges were created on both sides, and the Freemasons experienced the fastest growth over any time in history.

Nearly one-third of the presidents since Andrew Jackson have been Freemasons. When taking the oath of office, many presidents have sworn on the Bible used by George Washington in 1783.

AFTER THE WILLIAM MORGAN AFFAIR

William Morgan's body was never found. Some chose to believe that he had been given $500 to disappear into the Canadian wilderness. Others preferred testimony that indicated he had been dropped into the Niagara River with weights attached to his legs.

Reported sightings came in for several years. Wasn't he the man in Smyrna, Anatolia, wearing full Turkish garb, who claimed to be William Morgan? He was teaching English and French to the sultan's officials. But how did Morgan learn both French and Turkish to do this?

Perhaps he was the pirate in Havana, Cuba, who made such a confession just before his hanging? Or maybe the real William Morgan was living with the Mohawks out in the west? But wait. Others spotted him in Canada, Newfoundland, and Mexico. There was even a report of William Morgan in the Cayman Islands, married and with nine children.

Nothing could be verified except that William Morgan had disappeared.

As Freemasonry grew, several groups spun off, such as the

Shriners are often seen in parades, such as members on this Hospital for Children float in Pasadena, California. [Library of Congress]

Order of the Eastern Star, the Rainbow Girls, and the Shriners. The Shriners now have a network of twenty-two Shriners Hospitals for Children, where young patients are cared for regardless of their ability to pay.

In 1924, there were about three million members in the United States, but the number has declined since. Membership fell sharply in the 1960s, when the baby boomers became more interested in ending the Vietnam War and increasing civil rights. The decline continued with changing habits such as staying at home to watch television. There have also been a number of myths and conspiracy theories written about the Freemasons that cause more suspicion.

In 2015, U.S. membership dwindled to 1,161,253, with a loss of almost fifty thousand Grand Lodges. Some lodges are now gaining new members by hosting dinners where interested people can learn about Freemasonry. Women are also encouraged to join.

Today it is possible to find numerous books and internet sources that continue to reveal "secrets" of the Freemasons. But is it a "secret society" if they never change the secrets that can be discovered in so many places?

No Masonic incident like the William Morgan affair has occurred again. It was a tragedy of simmering fear and paranoia that limited freedom of speech, freedom of religion, and freedom to gather. Unfortunately, similar emotions continue to roil and rumble and threaten these precious rights today.

CHAPTER 6

Two Princes in the Tower of London

Over five hundred years ago,
a twelve-year-old boy, King Edward V of England,
and his nine-year-old brother, Richard,
disappeared from the Tower of London.
Were they murdered? Did they escape?
Through all these centuries their fate remains a mystery.

A CHAOTIC BACKGROUND

IT WAS MEDIEVAL ENGLAND, a time of knights and kings, princes and dukes, queens and princesses and lords. The royals, some from the House of Lancaster and others from the House of York, were related. They were fighting each other in a long series of civil wars called the Wars of the Roses. Each wanted to rule the kingdom and would use almost any means to gain power, including treason, torture, betrayal, beheading, or another bloody battle.

The Wars of the Roses came about because the Lancastrian king, Henry VI, was a very weak ruler. He was easily manipulated by his strong-willed queen, Margaret of Anjou.

In 1453, King Henry VI had a "sudden and thoughtless fright" when he did not recognize or react to others. The illness lasted for fifteen months, and Parliament appointed Richard, third duke of York, as protector of the realm. Margaret feared Richard would claim the throne over her infant son, Edward of Lancaster. When Henry VI recovered somewhat, Margaret persuaded him to dismiss Richard.

Richard immediately took up arms, and the Lancastrians and the Yorkists fought several battles for control over the next few years. In 1460, King Henry VI was captured, but he remained king and agreed to name Richard his heir over his own son, Edward of Lancaster. Margaret was hopping mad and intended to change the situation.

Two princes descending a staircase in the Tower of London.

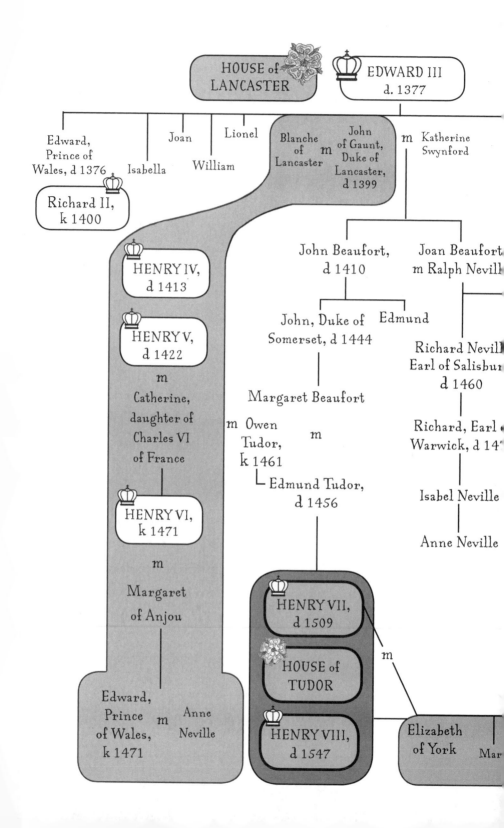

A PARTIAL GENEALOGY OF LANCASTER AND YORK

k: killed   d: died   m: married

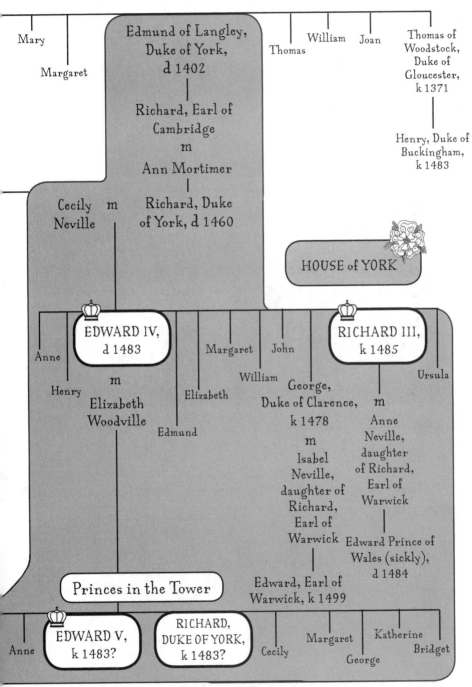

Mary

Margaret

Edmund of Langley,
Duke of York,
d 1402

Thomas   William   Joan

Thomas of
Woodstock,
Duke of
Gloucester,
k 1371

Richard, Earl of
Cambridge
m
Ann Mortimer

Henry, Duke of
Buckingham,
k 1483

Cecily   m   Richard, Duke
Neville   of York, d 1460

HOUSE of YORK

EDWARD IV,
d 1483

Margaret   John

RICHARD III,
k 1485

Anne

Henry

William

m

Elizabeth
Woodville

Elizabeth

Ursula

Edmund

George,
Duke of Clarence,
k 1478
m
Isabel
Neville,
daughter of
Richard,
Earl of
Warwick

m

Anne
Neville,
daughter
of Richard,
Earl of
Warwick

Edward Prince of
Wales (sickly),
d 1484

Edward, Earl of
Warwick, k 1499

Princes in the Tower

Anne

EDWARD V,
k 1483?

RICHARD,
DUKE OF YORK,
k 1483?

Cecily

Margaret   Katherine

George

Bridget

A fifteenth-century painting of the Tower of London, on the river Thames. [Wikimedia]

Henry had many Lancastrian supporters. Margaret managed to collect twenty thousand troops in Scotland and other areas north of London to challenge Richard. Richard took the best cannons out of the Tower of London and gathered five thousand men for combat, but he was outnumbered. On December 30, 1460, Margaret's

Lancastrians won the Battle of Wakefield. Richard was slain, as was his second son, Edmund, earl of Rutland.

Richard's eldest son, nineteen-year-old Edward, earl of March, was gifted in military strategy and ready for revenge. He marched into London and was proclaimed King Edward IV (the first Yorkist king of England) on March 4, 1461. A few weeks later, there was another clash with the queen's army in the Battle of Towton. During a terrible snowstorm, fifty thousand soldiers from both houses fought, and over twenty thousand people died.

King Edward IV won and kept his crown. The aging King Henry VI managed to flee to the mountains in Scotland. Margaret went into hiding with their son. That was not the last of Henry and Margaret.

BETRAYAL

King Edward IV was tall, handsome, and popular and was very effective at the beginning of his reign. He supported trade and the arts, but there were always threats to his claim to the throne.

King Henry VI was a particular challenge. After fleeing to Scotland, Henry was smuggled back into England and hid in various Lancastrian homes. When Edward IV heard about this, he and his allies tried to capture him.

Henry played hide-and-seek for more than a year. Once, at the last minute, he raced off and left behind his crown and a spoon. Then

From the House of Lancaster with the Red Rose

King Henry VI

Queen Margaret
of Anjou

Son Edward
of Lancaster

From the House of York with the White Rose

Richard, first duke
of York, grandfather
to the two princes

Edward of March
Eventually King Edward IV,
father to the two princes

A few royal players from the House of Lancaster and the House of York.

there were rumors that he was disguised as a monk. Finally he was arrested in 1465 as he attempted to hide in Clitheroe Wood.

Henry was marched back through London, where he was ridiculed with insults and injured by hurled garbage and stones. Then he was imprisoned in the Tower of London. His queen, Margaret, was in exile, but she did not stop plotting. She was always looking for ways to restore the crown to Henry and reclaim her son's line to the throne.

Meanwhile, King Edward IV needed an heir. In a secretive and stunning move, he married Elizabeth Woodville, a widow with two sons. At her urging, Edward began promoting her numerous relatives. Elizabeth's father, Richard Woodville, was made Earl of Rivers and became treasurer. Her son Thomas Grey married the king's niece and took on the title of Marquess of Dorset. Her other son became known as Sir Richard Grey. Her sister Catherine married Henry Stafford, duke of Buckingham. Other Woodville siblings made good marriages and gained much wealth and power. Many in the kingdom were not

Betrayers of King Edward IV

His brother George,
duke of Clarence

His former supporter
Richard Neville,
earl of Warwick

happy with this transfer of power. Just who were the Woodvilles anyway?

Eventually Edward IV and Elizabeth became the parents of three daughters, but as yet there was no male heir. Elizabeth was pregnant for the fourth time when her husband was trapped while camping and taken prisoner. He had been betrayed by his brother George, duke of Clarence, and Richard Neville, earl of Warwick. King Edward IV was taken to Warwick's castle. Those in charge of the coup could not control all the chaos, and King Edward IV was set free in October. However, Margaret and her now sixteen-year-old son returned from exile in Brittany to challenge him once again.

King Edward IV had lost too much of his army and supporters. He fled in such peril that he left behind his wife and family. His expensive coat of pine marten furs was the only thing he had left to purchase ship passage to escape. Many who served him were caught and beheaded.

Pregnant, Elizabeth fled the Tower of London with their young daughters and asked for sanctuary at Westminster Abbey, where they could be protected. Since the fifth century, this abbey had offered a safe place for criminals, debtors, and lawbreakers, but the queen did not mingle with them. She stayed in the house with the abbot.

Feeble Henry VI was restored to the throne. He was moved quickly from the prison to the opulent rooms of the Tower.

Safe for the time being in a sanctuary, Elizabeth gave birth to a son, Edward, four months later, on November 2, 1470.

Prince Edward,
the first of the two princes.

ROSES IN THE TOWER

These back-and-forth battles were part of the bloody Wars of the Roses. Both sides were related to each other as descendants of King Edward III, who had ruled from 1327 to 1377. For thirty years the House of York, represented by a white rose, and the House of Lancaster, with a red rose, would connive, betray, and murder each other to gain the crown.

A peek into the Tower of London would reveal which rose had won the latest battle.

The luxurious rooms would be occupied by the current rulers.

Medieval Weapons

Prisoners were stretched and tortured on the rack.

Iron caltrops were scattered across a battlefield
to maim the enemy knights and their horses.

Cannons were not used much
in the Wars of the Roses. They
were unreliable and could
blow up those nearby. Once improved,
cannons could crumble great stone
walls, and castles were no longer
good defenses.

Nicholas of the Tower
was the most important ship
in the royal fleet.

The losers most likely would be in the Tower prison, in the torture chambers, or perhaps beheaded at the executioner's block. Sometimes Tower rooms changed occupants overnight.

Whoever occupied the royal rooms had power, vast wealth, and exclusive access to the best weapons in the land. The Tower weapons were state-of-the-art and included chemical flamethrowers, racks that stretched and pulled victim's limbs with ropes, spiked caltrops to pierce horses' hooves, cannons, cord nets bristling with nails, the latest and best arrows by the thousands, and a huge warship known as *Nicholas of the Tower.*

While King Edward IV had the power, he had to be wary of brothers, uncles, cousins, Woodville in-laws, and various enemies and even friends who might want to take it away from him. He was especially leery of Queen Margaret. It was a tremendous job to keep his family safe and his heirs in line to inherit the crown.

THE HOUSE OF MAGNIFICENCE VERSUS A DOG AND A PET SPARROW

The deposed King Henry VI had been luckier than most when he lived in the prison part of the Tower. It was dark and mildewed but he had attendants, a priest for daily mass, and an allowance for velvet cloth to make his gowns and doublets. He continued to be feeble but enjoyed having a dog and a pet sparrow. There were also stories of a cat that came to visit, bringing an occasional pigeon to enrich his diet.

When King Edward IV was in power, he and his family had lived royally in the House of Magnificence. His luxurious Tower apartments consisted of three chambers. The first provided space for receiving visitors, such as other royalty and foreign envoys. The second area was an inner privy chamber for business affairs. And then there was the royal bedchamber. This third room was huge, with beds for six people to attend the king's needs. They followed an elaborate ritual to make his royal bed with linens, satin, and ermine, all sprinkled at the end with holy water.

RETURN OF EDWARD IV

King Edward IV was in exile when he was informed of the birth of his first son. Strengthened by the news, he was able to gather thirty-five ships of supporters and a thousand Yorkists hoping to return him to the throne. He sailed from a Dutch port toward England, but unfortunately a tremendous storm ruined his plans.

Later his brother Richard, duke of Gloucester, joined him. George, duke of Clarence, also turned his allegiance back to the king. Edward IV was able to raise another army of seven thousand men, and this time they retook the Tower. Edward IV moved into the royal rooms and once again sent deposed King Henry VI back to the prison.

Soon Edward IV was rejoined by Elizabeth with baby son Edward and daughters Elizabeth, Mary, and Cecily. They stayed in the Tower for safety because Margaret of Anjou and her son, Prince Edward of Lancaster, were always a threat.

MORE BLOODSHED IN THE FIGHT TO BE KING

Indeed, Margaret returned with an army in 1471, but she was defeated by King Edward IV. This time her seventeen-year-old son was killed, and Margaret was captured.

Henry VI was still a prisoner in the Tower. He was saddened to hear the news of his family. Henry hadn't seen his wife in many years, but she was on her way to the Tower as a prisoner. Just before she arrived, he died late at night. He may have been murdered by the king's youngest brother, Richard, duke of Gloucester, or at his command. Henry and Margaret never got to see each other again. Margaret was later ransomed by her cousin, King Louis XI of France. She died in poverty.

RAISING A PRINCE

This finally brings us to little Prince Edward. He was a baby, now out of sanctuary and living in the royal part of the Tower. His path to the throne seemed safe and clear as he advanced toward the age of fourteen. Should he inherit the kingdom before that age, he would require a protector.

His father named him Prince of Wales and Earl of Chester. The lady mistress of the nursery and a nurse took over his care. Sir Thomas Vaughan had the duty to carry him behind the king whenever there was a procession. At the king's insistence, forty-seven lords swore an oath that the young boy was "the very undoubted son and heir of our sovereign lord." Vaughan became a favorite companion and supporter of the little prince as he was growing up.

The king had a problem, however. How could he keep this vulnerable son safe while teaching him all the things he needed to know to be a king?

Sir Thomas Vaughan, once ransomed from French pirates by
Edward IV, was very faithful to the king and his son.

At age three, Prince Edward was sent off to live with Elizabeth's brother, Anthony Woodville, Lord Rivers, at Ludlow Castle in the Welsh Marches. This was a common practice for royal child-rearing. No women were at Ludlow, but the little prince had Sir Thomas Vaughan, a tutor, someone to handle finances, a military and exercise instructor, and knights for protection.

His father carefully planned out the daily schedule for young Edward.

- arise *"at a convenient hour according to his age"*
- attend *Matins and mass before breakfast*
- be instructed *"in such virtuous learning as his age will suffer to receive,"* including listening to *"such noble stories as behoveth a prince to understand and know"*

Ludlow Castle, where the young prince Edward was raised after age three.

- *spend afternoons in physical activity acquiring the knightly arts of horsemanship, swordmanship, and tossing the quintain*
- *after supper have some time for play*
- *go to bed at 8:00 p.m. (9:00 p.m. after he turned twelve)*
- *no "swearer, brawler, backbiter," was to be allowed into the household*

For nearly ten years, Prince Edward "devoted himself to horses and dogs and other useful exercises to invigorate his body." His uncle was kind, brave, and well educated and wrote charming poetry. Edward was very fond of him and Vaughan, and he lived a rich, warm, educated life. The young prince learned to understand verse and prose and was described as "remarkably gifted and well-advanced in learning for his twelve years."

THE SECOND PRINCE

On August 17, 1473, the king and queen had another son, Richard, duke of York. Over time they also had three more daughers. Five of their girls would reach adulthood: Elizabeth, Cecily, Anne, Katherine, and Bridget.

As was often done in these times, four-year-old Prince Richard was married to six-year-old Anne Mowbray, duchess of Norfolk, on January 15, 1478. Not too much is known about Richard's childhood,

Edward, earl of Warwick, son of George, duke of Clarence, was
orphaned and imprisoned in the Tower at age ten.

but he did not grow up with his brother. He apparently had quite a
musical talent and was described as "joyous and witty, nimble, and
ever ready for dances and games." With his marriage he gained the
dukedoms of Norfolk and Mowbray and all their fortunes. His young
bride died at age nine.

After the marriage, Edward IV charged his brother George, duke
of Clarence, with high treason because George had turned against
him again. Unlike many accused, who were often dragged from their
homes and hanged or beheaded without proof, Clarence was given a
trial and found guilty. He asked to determine his own means of death

and allegedly chose to drown in a rondolet of Malmsey wine. His wife had died recently, and it was agreed that his orphaned children, Margaret and Edward, earl of Warwick, would not inherit titles or land. All of George's wealth reverted to the crown, but later his son, Edward, would have a claim to the throne.

THE KING DIES, 1483

King Edward IV was living a very unhealthy life, indulging in too much food and drink and then vomiting so he could eat more, all "for the pleasure of gorging his stomach again." Then he got very sick.

As King Edward IV lay dying, possibly from pneumonia after a fishing trip, he decided to change his will. His son Prince Edward, now twelve, would need a protector until he turned fourteen and could rule on his own. In 1475, the king had written a will that entrusted the care of his sons to "our dearest wife the queen." This would have given Elizabeth and her greedy Woodville family tremendous wealth and power.

But at the very end Edward IV decided to name his thirty-one-year-old brother, Richard, duke of Gloucester, as the protector. Richard had been loyal to him when George had not. But did Edward consider that Richard had also been a participant in this violent age of civil war? That Richard had seen his father, two brothers, and many others killed? That he had been a ruthless bully, willing to kill to get his way?

At the time, Richard was governing England north of the river Trent. He had many loyal followers and avoided the Woodville court. This left a division of power between him and the queen's family. King Edward IV made a huge mistake by not unifying the rival factions of the Woodvilles and Richard. When the king died, this situation led to the tragedy of the young princes in the Tower.

TWO LETTERS IN ONE TERRIBLE DAY

Edward was two hundred miles away at Ludlow Castle when his father died on April 9, 1483. On April 11, 1483, the young prince was declared King Edward V in London, but neither he nor his uncle Lord Rivers were informed of either event.

Finally the young prince received two letters on April 14. One informed him of the death of his father, King Edward IV. By this time notables and royalty were already gathering for the funeral. The second letter was from his mother, telling him to be in London by May 1. The coronation was set for May 4. Lord Rivers decided to take two weeks for preparations. This delay was a costly mistake.

In London, Elizabeth had acted quickly. She ignored the new will and called upon the king's councillors to transfer the office of deputy constable of the Tower to her son, the Marquess of Dorset. They agreed. This meant Dorset was in charge of the king's treasures and all

Map of England and Wales during the Wars of the Roses.

the weapons in the Tower. She also tried to prevent Richard from becoming the protector by arranging a quick coronation for her son.

The councillors met in London, and all agreed that "the Prince should succeed his father in all his glory" but that the protectorate should go to Richard, the only living brother of Edward IV. In a separate issue they appointed Elizabeth's youngest brother, Sir Edward Woodville, admiral of the fleet. He had orders to take the navy and control the French pirates off the coast.

Richard, duke of Gloucester, was two hundred miles away in Yorkshire at Middleham Castle. No one told him of the death of his brother until Lord Hastings, King Edward IV's best friend, sent him an urgent note. The queen, he warned, meant to oust him.

Richard held a funeral ceremony for his brother and had all the nobility take an oath of loyalty to the new young king. Then he went to work on his own plan for power and wealth.

He wrote to the prince, now proclaimed King Edward V, saying that he and the Duke of Buckingham would meet him in Northampton. Each would bring an army of three hundred supporters to travel with the king to London. Together they would make a more magnificent entry into the city. Lord Rivers agreed.

ANOTHER BETRAYAL

When Edward V and his attendants reached Northampton on April 29, 1483, Lord Rivers decided the town wasn't big enough for all the people coming. He had his troops camp in the surrounding

Richard, duke of
Gloucester, youngest brother
of King Edward IV

Henry Stafford,
duke of Buckingham

Anthony Woodville,
Lord Rivers

Lord Hastings,
best friend of
King Edward IV

Whom can the young King Edward V trust?

area and took the king fourteen miles south to Stony Stratford to stay at the Rose and Crown Inn.

When Richard and Buckingham arrived to find the king gone, Richard used this change to justify a new plot twist. Lord Rivers returned to explain the move over a nice dinner, but Richard had other plans. Lord Rivers and his companions found themselves locked in the Northampton Inn as prisoners.

Richard and Buckingham continued on to Stony Stratford early in the morning. Richard bowed before the king and said his father's death was the fault of the Woodvilles, who ruined his health. Then he said that Lord Rivers was accused of treason and had been arrested.

Edward was not convinced of any treason and "wept and was nothing content." But he eventually surrendered his care to his uncle Richard. No blood was shed, but at this point, after twenty years of being in control, the Woodvilles lost the power game.

When the queen heard this news, she fled with nine-year-old Richard and her daughters to the sanctuary of Westminster Abbey. She had loyal servants pack crates and boxes with Tower treasures and drag them off in the darkness of night. A great hole was ripped in the sanctuary wall so the treasures could be quickly hauled inside.

While rumors raced through London like wildfire, the Woodvilles lodged once again in the abbot's house, where Edward V had been born. Richard's servants filled the river Thames with boats to prevent the queen or anyone from leaving the house. Needless to say, the coronation of the young king was delayed.

But the queen still had a few cards to play. She had a vast royal treasure. And her brother Sir Edward Woodville was in charge of the naval fleet. Richard took steps to get the ships returned, but Sir Edward managed to keep two ships and sailed off to Brittany to join a young relative of Henry VI, also named Henry. He had been living in exile but could make a claim to the throne.

A FEW WEEKS AS KING EDWARD V

On May 4, King Edward V marched into London wearing blue velvet, an expensive material reserved for the royal family. His uncle Richard was on his right, Buckingham on his left, both wearing black cloth. Citizens and magnates swore loyalty to Edward, and then he was taken to the royal apartments of the Tower. He had a room with birds and angels in gold and vermilion painted on the walls.

Richard was proclaimed protector of the king, a temporary title that would lapse at Edward V's coronation, now scheduled for June. During this time the council gave Richard power "just like another king" and also "the tutelage and oversight of the king's most royal person." But the councillors criticized him for accusing Lord Rivers and others of treason and for not seeing to the safety of the queen.

Richard tried to get the queen and her family to leave sanctuary and encouraged people to visit her. He also held secret meetings to strengthen his plans to change the royal situation.

Two princes at the Tower windows.

Meanwhile, Edward V learned the business of being king. He signed documents and proclamations issued in his name. Richard the protector signed documents as "brother and uncle of kings."

Buckingham was rewarded with fifty castles for his role in the events. But some were starting to worry about the safety of the young king. Why were his relatives and supporters being held in prison? Unease spread "like mist at Westminster and the Tower." The mood became one of "dark corners and the rustle of whispers," according to Richard III biographer Paul Murray Kendall.

RICHARD MAKES HIS MOVE

Richard knew he would lose his high office after the coronation and realized he must have the other prince, nine-year-old Richard, duke of York, in his power. For three weeks the queen refused to leave sanctuary. Richard the protector raised a York army in the north. Those loyal to the king were executed without a trial. He gave orders to execute the queen's brother Lord Rivers, her son Sir Richard Grey, and Lord Hastings, King Edward IV's best friend.

Richard then sent agents into the streets shouting "Treason! Treason!" and proclaiming that these people were plotting to kill him. All were innocent but were executed without a trial or witnesses. In another twist, Richard implied that the marriage of Edward IV to Elizabeth Woodville was not valid because Edward had earlier promised to marry another. Therefore, none of his children were entitled to inherit the throne. This gave Richard a stronger claim to the throne.

Little Edward of Warwick, the eight-year-old son of the late George, duke of Clarence, had a good claim to the throne also. Richard kept him hidden in the household of his wife, Anne Neville.

Plans for the crowning of Edward V were abandoned. Richard stopped wearing black and starting wearing the royal color purple.

Under force, nine-year-old Richard, duke of York, was taken from sanctuary to join his brother in the Tower. The boys were moved from the royal apartments to the Garden Tower (now called the Bloody

Tower), which had a garden where the boys could play. For a time they enjoyed a small zoo, shot arrows, and pursued other amusements. They were occasionally seen at the Tower windows, but there was only one sighting of the boys in public after this.

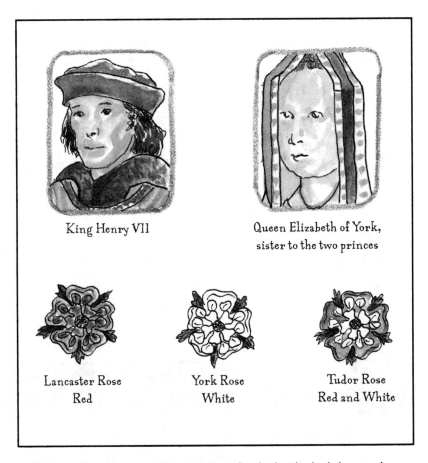

King Henry VII

Queen Elizabeth of York, sister to the two princes

Lancaster Rose
Red

York Rose
White

Tudor Rose
Red and White

When a Tudor King, Henry VII, married a Yorkist bride, Elizabeth, he united two conflicting families in the Wars of the Roses.

Then the situation for the young king got much worse. His thirteen familiar attendants were barred from the Tower and replaced by a few hired by Richard. The boys were now prisoners. On June 25, 1483, Richard became King Richard III, and Edward V's short time as ruler of the kingdom was over.

When Edward was told that his uncle had taken his throne, he sighed. "Alas, I would my uncle would let me have my life yet, though I lose my kingdom." Soon even the servants hired by Richard were removed, and only Dr. John Argentine was allowed to visit the boys. He found Edward depressed, unwashed, praying, and in pain from a bone disease or tooth decay in his jaw.

By early September 1483, the princes simply disappeared and were never seen again. Later came reports of two ghostly boys holding hands on the stairs.

King Richard III's only child, Edward of Middleham, became Prince of Wales on September 8. This royal title had just recently belonged to the missing Edward V. Unfortunately this child was sickly and died within a year at the age of ten.

MORE BATTLES

The Duke of Buckingham was shocked by these events. He tried to start a revolt against Richard by uniting the rival York and Lancaster families behind Henry Tudor, the nephew of Henry VI. Henry Tudor had spent his life in flight, exile, and hairbreadth escapes to survive as the last Lancastrian descendant of Edward III.

Richard's huge spy system discovered the plot. Buckingham was captured in a terrible storm and beheaded. Off the coast in the same storm, Henry decided to retreat to Brittany and put off his invasion. Anticipating another battle with Henry, Richard told gunsmiths from Flanders to make the Serpentine, an extra-long, thin cannon mounted on a pivot to increase the range of its four-pound shot.

Sure enough, Henry Tudor returned in 1485 and landed in Wales with an army raised in France. By this time no one liked or trusted Richard. There was more combat, and Richard III's allies deserted him. He was killed at the Battle of Bosworth. A gold coronet from his helmet was placed on Henry's head, and he became King Henry VII.

This ended the Wars of the Roses and started the reign of the Tudors. Henry had a Tudor rose designed that was a blend of red and white to symbolize a new beginning. In another gesture of unity, Henry married Elizabeth of York in January 1486. She was the eldest daughter of Edward IV, the sister of the two missing princes.

PRETENDERS TO THE THRONE

Meanwhile, many were still alarmed and saddened by the disappearance of the two young boys, always referred to through the centuries

Perkin Warbeck   Lambert Simnel

Two serious pretenders to the throne of England.

as the two princes. With no bodies, no funerals, and no explanation, there was plenty of room for theories to explain the loss. Were they poisoned? Drowned in wine? Were they concealed in a box and dropped into the sea? If they were killed, who gave the orders? Or maybe they survived somewhere in exile? Did they have secret new identities?

Since there were no answers, young men began to make claims to the throne. None impersonated Edward, probably because he was better known. But several pretenders claimed to be Richard of York or his cousin Edward of Warwick, who could each make a claim for the crown if still alive.

One of these was Lambert Simnel, a ten-year-old baker boy. With the help of a Yorkist priest named Richard Symonds, he claimed to be Edward, earl of Warwick, the young boy who had been taken to live with Richard III's wife: the nephew of King Edward IV and son of George, duke of Clarence.

The real Warwick had been a prisoner in the Tower, but a rumor existed that he had escaped. Simnel was well tutored in the ways of a king and was described as "a boy so learned, that, had he ruled, he would have as a learned man."

Simnel had supporters in Ireland, and in Dublin he was crowned King Edward VI. He became the figurehead for a Yorkist rebellion in 1487. Warwick's aunt, Margaret of York, the duchess of Burgundy, sent two thousand Flemish and Irish soldiers for support, but Henry defeated them.

King Henry VII pardoned young Simnel because he felt the boy had been used by the participants in the plot to overthrow him. Simnel was given a job in the royal kitchens as a spit-turner and then became a falconer.

Several years later another handsome youth showed up, claiming to be the younger prince, Richard, duke of York. He also had the support of Margaret, the duchess of Burgundy, and knew a great deal about royal behavior. This man, Perkin Warbeck, was the right age, with similar looks. He also had an exceptional musical talent like Richard.

Warbeck claimed to have been allowed to escape when his older brother was murdered. He was very believable and convinced many of the sovereigns of Europe, including at one point Charles VIII of France and the Holy Roman Emperor Maximilian I.

After six years of this masquerade, Warbeck deserted some supporters before a battle and surrendered. He was eventually imprisoned in the Tower. The real Warwick was also there as a prisoner, and when they were caught in a plot to overthrow Henry VII, the king had them both executed.

The disappearance of the two young princes remained a mystery.

WHAT ABOUT THE BONES?

Several years later Sir Thomas More wrote about a possible conclusion to the fate of young Edward and Richard. The story came from Sir James Tyrell after extreme torture on the rack. He was the knight of the body in the Tower. This meant that he slept on a pallet outside the royal bedchamber to guarantee the king a good night's sleep.

According to Tyrell, Sir Robert Brackenbury, newly appointed constable of the Tower, was told that Richard III wanted the princes dead. Brackenbury refused to do it, and Buckingham ended his support of the king. So the order went to Sir James Tyrell, who said he hired two others to do the job.

In his telling, the men entered the Garden Tower sometime in September and suffocated the boys in their soft feather beds. Then the bodies were buried at the foot of a staircase under a heap of stones. Later an order was given to move them. But did this happen? And did

Richard give the order? Or was it Henry? Or did the boys really survive?

In 1674, almost two centuries later, King Charles II decided to fix up the old Tower. Under a staircase, workers found a wooden chest with the remains of a child four feet ten and another four feet six and a half. They also found wisps of blue velvet with the bodies. Since this material was only invented by the Italians in the fourteenth century and was too expensive for all but royalty, this clue ruled out other children who disappeared in the earliest centuries of the Tower, which had been built in 1066.

The skeletons were put on display, and souvenir hunters snatched up some bones. The remains were then sent to a museum in Oxford, where more bones disappeared, replaced by animal bones. Finally, in 1678, the skeletons were buried at Westminster Abbey.

In 1933, experts examined the remains, removing all the animal bones. The skeletons came from two slim young children. One was between eleven and thirteen (Edward was twelve years, eleven months) and showed signs of dental or jaw disease. The other was between nine and eleven (Richard was nine). They were not, however, able to tell if the children were male or female because of their young age. The bones were reburied.

No modern DNA tests or other analysis have been allowed to confirm if these are the two young princes, so many theories still exist about their fate. Theories come with expressions like "it may have been," "evidence suggests," "someone said," "very near to the truth."

Although people have spent five hundred years looking for an answer, it is still not possible to know the absolute truth about what happened to the two young princes in the Tower. Their story has passed from ancient history into folklore, ghost stories, and new looks at old theories.

BIBLIOGRAPHY

CHAPTER 1 / MISSING! 1975
JIMMY HOFFA AND THE TRUCKERS

Brandt, Charles. *"I Heard You Paint Houses": Frank "the Irishman" Sheeran and the Inside Story of the Mafia, the Teamsters, and the Last Ride of Jimmy Hoffa.* Hanover, NH: Steerforth, 2004.

Hoffa, James R. *Hoffa: The Real Story.* With Oscar Fraley. New York: Stein and Day, 1975.

———. *The Trials of Jimmy Hoffa: An Autobiography.* With Donald I. Rogers. Chicago: Henry Regnery, 1970.

Kennedy, Robert F. *The Enemy Within.* New York: Harper & Row, 1960.

Russell, Thaddeus. *Out of the Jungle: Jimmy Hoffa and the Remaking of the American Working Class.* New York: Knopf, 2001.

Sheridan, Walter. *The Fall and Rise of Jimmy Hoffa.* New York: Saturday Review, 1972.

Zuberi, Tukufu, Wes Cowan, and Kaiama Glover. "Who Killed Jimmy Hoffa?" *History Detectives Special Investigations.* PBS, 2014. pbs.org/opb /historydetectives/investigation/who-killed-jimmy-hoffa.

CHAPTER 2 / MISSING! 1971
D. B. COOPER, DOWN, DOWN, DOWN, AND GONE

Gray, Geoffrey. *Skyjack: The Hunt for D. B. Cooper.* New York: Crown, 2011.

Gunther, Max. *D. B. Cooper: What Really Happened.* Chicago: Contemporary Books, 1985.

Federal Bureau of Investigation. "D. B. Cooper." FBI Records: The Vault. vault .fbi.gov/D-B-Cooper%20.

History Channel. *D. B. Cooper: Case Closed?* July 12, 2016.

Kaye, Tom, Alan Stone, and Carol Abraczinskas. "McCrone Labs Analysis 2017." The Hunt for D. B. Cooper. CitizenSleuths.com.

Lacitis, Erik. "Does That Evidence Truly Tie D. B. Cooper to Boeing? Plot Thickens." *Seattle Times*. Jan. 20, 2017. seattletimes.com/seattle-news /northwest/does-that-evidence-truly-tie-db-cooper-to-boeing-plot -thickens.

Rhodes, Bernie. *D. B. Cooper: The Real McCoy*. With Russell P. Calame. Salt Lake City: University of Utah Press, 1991.

Streissguth, Tom. *The D. B. Cooper Hijacking*. Mankato, MN: Child's World, 2015.

Tosaw, Richard T. *D. B. Cooper: Dead or Alive? The True Story of the Legendary Skyjacker*. Ceres, CA: Tosaw Publishing, 1984.

CHAPTER 3 / MISSING! 1939
BARBARA FOLLETT, A CHILD AUTHOR

Cooke, Stefan, ed. *Barbara Newhall Follett: A Life in Letters*. Self-published, Farksolia, 2015.

Follett, Barbara. *The House Without Windows and Eepersip's Life There*. New York: Knopf, 1927.

[Follett, Wilson]. "To a Daughter, One Year Lost." *Atlantic Monthly*, May 1941.

Forbes, Malcolm. *What Happened to Their Kids? Children of the Rich and Famous*. With Jeff Bloch. New York: Simon and Schuster, 1990.

McCurdy, Harold Grier, ed. *Barbara: The Unconscious Autobiography of a Child Genius*. With Helen Follett. Chapel Hill: University of North Carolina Press, 1966.

CHAPTER 4 / MISSING! 1937
AMELIA EARHART, THE LOST LEGEND

Adler, Jerry. "The Lady Vanishes (Again)." *Smithsonian*, January 2015, 34–41.

Amelia Earhart at Purdue. Purdue University Libraries E-Archives. earchives.lib .purdue.edu/cdm/collections.

Amelia Earhart Papers (George Palmer Putnam Collection). Purdue University Libraries E-Archives. earchives.lib.purdue.edu/cdm/collections.

Backus, Jean, ed. *Letters From Amelia, 1901–1937.* Boston: Beacon Press, 1982.

Brandenburg, Bob. "Analysis of Radio Direction Finder Bearings in the Search for Amelia Earhart." The Earhart Project, Aug. 2006. tighar.org /Projects/Earhart/Archives/Research/ResearchPapers/Brandenburg /RDFResearch/DFpaper.htm.

Brink, Randall. *Lost Star: The Search for Amelia Earhart.* New York: W. W. Norton, 1993.

Campbell, Mike. *Amelia Earhart: The Truth at Last*, second edition. Camp Hill, PA: Sunbury Press, 2016.

Earhart, Amelia. *The Fun of It: Random Records of My Flying and of Women in Aviation.* New York: Harcourt Brace, 1975.

———. *Last Flight.* New York: Harcourt Brace, 1937.

———. *20 Hrs. 40 Min.: Our Flight in the* Friendship. Washington, D.C.: National Geographic Adventure Classics, 2003.

Encyclopedia Britannica. s.v. "Amelia Earhart," Nov. 15, 2017. britannica.com /biography/Amelia-Earhart.

Fleming, Candace. *Amelia Lost: The Life and Disappearance of Amelia Earhart.* New York: Schwartz & Wade Books, 2011.

Gillespie, Ric. *Finding Amelia: The True Story of the Earhart Disappearance.* Annapolis, MD: Naval Institute Press, 2006.

The History Channel. *Amelia Earhart: The Lost Evidence.* July 9, 2017. history.com /specials/amelia-earhart-the-lost-evidence.

International Group for Historic Aircraft Recovery. "The Earhart Project." tighar .org/Projects/Earhart/AEdescr.html.

Sherman, Stephen. "Amelia Earhart: Aviatrix Lost Over the Pacific." Acepilots .com, Sept. 26, 2012. acepilots.com/earhart.html.

CHAPTER 5 / MISSING! 1826
WILLIAM MORGAN AND A BOOK OF SECRETS

Henry, Jacques. *Mozart the Freemason: The Masonic Influence on His Musical Genius.* Translated by Jack Cain. Rochester, VT: Inner Traditions, 2006.

Hodapp, Christopher. *Freemasons for Dummies.* Hoboken, NJ: John Wiley & Sons, 2013.

Kaplan, Fred. *John Quincy Adams: American Visionary.* New York: HarperCollins, 2014.

Kinney, Jay. *The Masonic Myth: Unlocking the Truth About the Symbols, the Secret Rites, and the History of Freemasonry.* New York: HarperCollins, 2009.

Ridley, Jasper. *The Freemasons: A History of the World's Most Powerful Secret Society.* New York: Arcade, 2001.

Stavish, Mark. *Freemasonry: Rituals, Symbols & History of the Secret Society.* Woodbury, MN: Llewellyn, 2007.

Vaughn, William Preston. *The Antimasonic Party in the United States, 1826–1843.* Louisville: University Press of Kentucky, 1983.

Whitelaw, Nancy. *Andrew Jackson: Frontier President.* Greensboro, NC: Morgan Reynolds, 2001.

CHAPTER 6 / MISSING! 1483
TWO PRINCES IN THE TOWER OF LONDON

Ashdown-Hill, John. *The Wars of the Roses.* Gloucestershire, UK: Amberley Publishing, 2015.

Ashley, Mike. *A Brief History of British Kings and Queens.* New York: Carroll and Graf, 2002.

Baldwin, David. *Elizabeth Woodville: Mother of the Princes in the Tower.* Gloucestershire, UK: Sutton, 2002.

Fisher, Leonard Everett. *Tower of London.* New York: Macmillan, 1987.

Jones, Dan. *The Wars of the Roses: The Fall of the Plantagenets and the Rise of the Tudors.* New York: Penguin, 2015.

Jones, Nigel. *Tower: An Epic History of the Tower of London.* New York: St. Martin's Press, 2011.

Riley, Gail Blasser. *Tower of London: England's Ghostly Castle.* New York: Bearport, 2007.

Weir, Alison. *The Princes in the Tower.* New York: Random House, 1992.

———. *The Wars of the Roses.* New York: Ballantine Books, 1995.

INDEX

Index

Index

Index

Index

ships, 90–91
  America, 122
  Carnegie, *92*, 94, *95*
Shriners, *184*
Simnel, Lambert, 216–17
slavery, 175, 177, 182
Snook, Neta, 115–17
Sperry, Armstrong, 99
Spindel, Bernard, *28*
St. John, Edward Porter, 69, 80, 82, 83, 89–90
Stafford, Henry, Duke of Buckingham, 193–94, 207–15
strawberries, 11–12
strikebreakers, 15
strikes, 10–11, 15–18
Stultz, Bill, 121
Syrian Mothers' Club, 119

The Three Mulla-Mulgars (de laMare), 75
Trail of Tears, 180
truck drivers, 16
  diseases and, *19*
  Hoffa talking to, *14*
  unionizing of, 10–19
20 Hrs. 40 mins (Earhart), 126
typewriter
  fascination with, 65
  Follett at, *62*

unemployment, 11
unions, 10–19

Vaughan, Thomas, *200*
The Velveteen Rabbit (Bianco), 91
The Voyage of the Norman D. (Follett), 91

Warbeck, Perkin, 216–18
Wars of the Roses, 187, 195, *206*, 213–15
Washington, George, *169*, 170, 183
weapons, medieval, *196*
Weed, Thurlow, *177*, 178
wiretapping, *28*
Wirt, William, 181–82
women
  education for, 135
  equality for, 126
Woodville, Elizabeth, 193–95, 199, 205
World War I, 112, 114
World War II, 107

York, House of, 187, *188–89*, *192*, 214–15

Zerilli, Anthony, 33